Shortcut to
Italian

The 100 Words You Need to Speak
over 500 Italian Phrases

Berlitz Publishing
New York   Munich   Singapore

Contacting the Editors
Every effort has been made to provide accurate information in this publication, but changes are inevitable. The publisher cannot be responsible for any resulting loss, inconvenience or injury. We would appreciate it if readers would call our attention to any errors or outdated information by contacting Berlitz Publishing, 193 Morris Avenue, Springfield, NJ 07081, USA.
email: comments@berlitzbooks.com

Original Edition: 2006 by Berlitz Publishing, Munich

Berlitz Trademark Reg. U.S. Patent Office and other countries. Marca Registrada. Used under license from Berlitz Investment Corporation

Second Printing: February 2007

Printed in Singapore

Author: Alexandra Desbalmes

Illustrations: Katrin Merle

Cover Photo: Jupiter Images Corporation

Editorial: Emily Bernath, Duccio Faggella, Christopher Gross, Christiane Heil, Juergen Lorenz

Production: Elizabeth Gaynor, Blair Swick

Contents

How to Use This Book

You need only to memorize 100 Italian words in order to speak over 500 of the most useful phrases. To take full advantage of this concept please follow these simple steps:

- Memorize the vocabulary in the **100 Words section** in the beginning of the book. The words have been organized in groups to make it easier for you to memorize them. You'll notice that the verbs listed in the 100 Words section aren't fully conjugated. You'll need only the verb forms listed in this book to make 500+ phrases.

- You memorize only 100 words but your basic vocabulary actually consists of more since you are able to create compound words. The important ones are also listed in the **100 Words section**, others will be explained in tip boxes or footnotes. The abbreviation for singular is *sing.*, for plural *pl.*, for formal *form.* and informal *inform.* Masculine forms are indicated by ♂, feminine forms by ♀.

- The **100 Words section** as well as each individual chapter contain **Language Tip** boxes in red explaining important rules with examples.

- **Cultural Tips**, in green, inform you about important customs and traditions in Italy.

- The chapters are organized by topics, e.g. Accommodations. Each chapter provides you with the basic and most useful expressions to function in a variety of situations. At times, phrases are supplemented by illustrations.

- The **Dictionary** in the back of the book gives you all the Italian words and expressions used in this program.

- The phonetic system used in this book makes it easy to pronounce the Italian words. Simply read the words as you would read them in English.

Pronunciation

Consonants

Letter	Approximate Pronunciation	Example
c	1) before e and i, like *ch* in *chip* 2) elsewhere, like *c* in *cat*	**cerco** **conto**
ch	like *c* in *cat*	**che**
g	1) before e and i, like *j* in *jet* 2) elsewhere, like *g* in *go*	**valigia** **grande**
gh	like *g* in *go*	**ghiaccio**
gl	like *lli* in *million*	**gli**
gn	like *ni* in *onion*	**bagno**
h	always silent	**ha**
r	trilled like a Scottish *r*	**deriva**
s	1) generally like *s* in *sit* 2) sometimes like *z* in *zoo*	**questo** **viso**
sc	1) before e and i, like *sh* in *shut* 2) elsewhere, like *sk* in *skin*	**uscita** **scarpa**
z/zz	1) generally like *ts* in *hits* 2) sometimes like *ds* in *roads*	**grazie** **romanzo**

B, d, f, k, l, m, n, p, q, t and **v** are pronounced as in English.

Vowels

a	like *a* in *father*	**casa**
e	1) can always be pronounced like *ay* in *way*, but without moving tongue or lips	**sera**
	2) sometimes pronounced like *e* in *get* or, when long, more like *ai* in *hair*	**bello**

Letter	Approximate Pronunciation	Example
i	like *ee* in *meet*	**vini**
o	like *o* in *go*	**sole**
u	1) like *oo* in *foot*	**fumo**
	2) like *w* in *well*	**buono**

Two or More Vowels

In groups of vowels **a, e** and **o** are strong; **i** and **u** are weak vowels. The following combinations occur:

two strong vowels	pronounced as two separate syllables	**beato**
a stong vowel and a weak vowel	1) the weak one is pronounced more quickly and with less stress than the strong one; such sounds are diphthongs and constitute only one syllable	**piede**
	2) if the weak vowel is stressed, it is pronounced as a separate syllable	**due**
two weak vowels	pronounced as a diphthong; generally the second one is stressed more	**guida**

100 Words

1	**sì** see	yes
2	**no** noh	no
3	**e** eh	and
4	**non** nohn	not

Language Tip

The negation most often used in Italian is *non*. It always precedes the conjugated verb and can simply be translated as "not".

5	**il** eel	the
	lo loh	the; him, it *pronoun*
	i ♀ ee	the *pl.*

Language Tip

The definite article *il* becomes *lo* if the masculine noun starts with *gn, ps, x, z* or *s + consonant*.

6	**la** lah	the; she *sing.*
	La lah	you *sing. form.*
	le ♂ leh	the *pl.*; you *pl.*; them; their

7 **un** ♂ oon   a
   una ♀ <u>oo</u>nah   a
   l'una ♀ <u>loo</u>nah   one o'clock

Language Tip

Italian has two genders: masculine and feminine. The male definite article is *il* and the indefinite article is *un*, while the female articles are *la* and *una*.

Before a vowel the definite article always becomes *l'* (as in *l'ora* = the hour), whether the noun is masculine or feminine. Likewise the feminine form of the indefinite article changes to *un'* (*un'ora* = an hour) if followed by a vowel.

---

8 **mi** me   me; to me
   me meh   me *stressed*
9 **ti** tee   you; to you *sing. inform.*
   te teh   you *stressed sing. inform.*

10 **tuo** <u>too</u>-oh   your(s) *sing. inform.*

11 **si** see   one; oneself

12 **suo** <u>soo</u>-oh   his/her(s)/its;
                       your(s) *sing. form.*

13 **noi** <u>noh</u>-ee   we; us *stressed*

14 **voi** <u>voh</u>-ee   your(s) *stressed, pl.*

15 **vi** vee   (to) you *pl.*

16 **vostro** <u>voh</u>stroh — your *pl.*

17 **ci** chee — us; to us; there; to

Language Tip

Possessive pronouns agree in gender (male or female) and number (singular or plural) with the noun they modify: *la tua camera* (your room), *il tuo regalo* (your present), *i vostri biglietti* (your tickets), *le vostre camere* (your rooms).
Generally only the last letter of the pronoun changes. The singular is *vostro* ♂ and *vostra* ♀ and the plural is *vostri* ♂ and *vostre* ♀. Note that in Italian the possessive pronoun is still preceded by the article, as the examples above show.

---

18 **Ciao!** <u>chah</u>-oh — Hello!/Good-bye!

19 **Buongiorno.** bwohn-<u>johr</u>noh — Good day./Good morning.

20 **Arrivederci.** ahr-reeveh-<u>dehr</u>chee — Good-bye.

21 **Scusi.** <u>skoo</u>zee — Excuse me./I am sorry.
   Scusa. <u>skoo</u>zah — Excuse me. *sing. inform.*
   Scusate. skoo<u>zah</u>-teh — Excuse me. *pl.*
   Scusi? <u>skoo</u>zee — Excuse me?
   (I beg your pardon?)

22 **Grazie.** <u>grah</u>tzee-eh — Thank you.

23	**cosa** <u>koh</u>zah	what
	la cosa lah <u>koh</u>zah	cause, thing
24	**come** <u>koh</u>meh	how
25	**quando** <u>kwahn</u>doh	when; if
26	**quanto** <u>kwahn</u>toh	how much
27	**quale** <u>kwah</u>leh	which
	quali <u>kwah</u>lee	which *pl.*
	qualcuno kwahl-<u>koo</u>noh	someone
	qualcosa kwahl-<u>koh</u>zah	something
28	**dove** <u>doh</u>veh	where; where to

Language Tip

The word *dove* (where) can be found in the expression *dov'è* (where is). For easier pronunciation the *e* is dropped from *dove* as in *Dov'è il regalo?* (Where's the present?) To ask about more than one item, you say: *Dove sono i biglietti?* (Where are the tickets?)

The same applies to the words *come* (com'è = how is), *cosa* (cos'è = what is) and *quale* (qual'è = which is).

29	**che** keh	which; who; that; as
30	**qui** kwee	here
31	**questo** <u>kweh</u>stoh	this (one)

32	**quello** <u>kwehl</u>-loh	that (one)
33	**tutto** <u>toot</u>-toh	all; whole
34	**due** <u>doo</u>-eh	two
35	**più** pew	more
36	**molto** <u>mohl</u>toh	much; very
37	**tanto** <u>tahn</u>toh	a lot; so much
38	**troppo** <u>trohp</u>-poh	too (much)
39	**niente** nee-<u>ehn</u>teh	nothing
40	**altro** <u>ahl</u>troh	another

Language Tip

The feminine and the plural forms of *quanto* (how much), *questo* (this), *tutto* (all), *molto* (many), *tanto* (so much), *troppo* (too much) and *altro* (another) are formed the same way as most Italian adjectives. Replace the *-o* at the end of the masculine form with an *-a* to change to the feminine form (e.g. *questa* = this one). To form the masculine plural, replace the *-o* with an *-i*, (e.g. *questi* = "these") or for the feminine plural with an *-e* (e.g. *queste* = "these").

41	**ieri** ee-<u>eh</u>ree	yesterday
42	**oggi** <u>ohdj</u>ee	today
43	**domani** doh<u>mah</u>-nee	tomorrow
44	**ora** <u>oh</u>rah **l'ora** ♂ <u>loh</u>rah	now hour; time

45	**subito** <u>soo</u>beetoh	immediately
46	**ancora** ahn<u>koh</u>rah	still; yet
47	**tardi** <u>tahr</u>dee	late
48	**a** ah	to; at
	alle <u>ahl</u>-leh	at (time)
49	**con** kohn	with
50	**per** pehr	for; to; in order to
51	**in** een	in; on; at
52	**di** dee	from; out; for; as
53	**da** dah	to; from; since
54	**ma** mah	but
55	**la mattina** lah maht-<u>tee</u>nah	morning
56	**il giorno** eel <u>john</u>noh	day
57	**la sera** lah <u>seh</u>rah	evening
	stasera stah-<u>seh</u>rah	this evening
58	**la notte** lah <u>noht</u>-te	night
59	**il tempo** eel <u>tehm</u>poh	time; weather
60	**il nome** eel <u>noh</u>meh	name
61	**la camera** lah <u>kah</u>mehrah	room
62	**il letto** eel <u>leht</u>-toh	bed
	il lettino eel leht-<u>tee</u>noh	children's bed
63	**il pasto** eel <u>pah</u>stoh	meal
64	**il biglietto** eel bee-<u>lyeht</u>-toh	ticket

65 **la taglia** lah <u>tah</u>lya   size (clothes)

66 **il regalo** eel reh<u>gah</u>loh   gift; present

67 **Stati Uniti d'America***   United States of America
<u>stah</u>tee oo<u>nee</u>tee
dah<u>meh</u>-reekah

Language Tip

Most words ending in -o are masculine and most words ending in -a are feminine. Words ending in -e can be either masculine or feminine.

To make a masculine noun plural, replace the o or e at the end of the word with an i (biglietto – biglietti, nome – nomi). For feminine nouns, replace the a with an e. If the feminine word ends in an e, it is replaced with an i in the plural (camera – camere, notte – notti).

---

68 **bene** <u>beh</u>neh   good *adverb*
   meglio <u>meh</u>lyoh   better

69 **male** <u>mah</u>leh   bad *adverb*

70 **buon(o)** bwohn (<u>bwoh</u>noh)   good

71 **bel(lo)** behl (<u>behl</u>-loh)   nice, pretty
   bellissimo   wonderful
   behl-<u>lees</u>-seemoh

---

* Other English-speaking countries:
   Gran-Bretagna grahn breh<u>tah</u>nyah Great Britain
   Canada kah-nah-<u>dah</u>   Canada

Language Tip

If the adjectives *buono* (good) and *bello* (nice) come before a masculine noun, they will generally be shortened to *buon* and *bel*.

72	**brutto** <u>broot</u>-toh	ugly
73	**grande** <u>grahn</u>deh	large; big
74	**piccolo** <u>peak</u>-kohloh	small
75	**pronto** <u>prohn</u>toh	ready
76	**vicino** vee<u>chee</u>noh	near; nearby
77	**caro** <u>kah</u>roh	expensive; precious
78	**rotto** <u>roht</u>-toh	broken

Language Tip

In Italian, adjectives always agree in gender and number with the noun they modify: *il regalo piccolo* (the small present) or *la camera piccola* (the small room).
To emphasize the adjective, or when forming the comparative, add the word *più*, as in *caro* (expensive), *più caro* (more expensive), *il più caro* (most expensive).

79 **essere** eh<u>s</u>-sehreh   to be
  sono <u>soh</u>noh   I am; they are
  sei say   you are *sing. inform.*
  è eh   he/she/it is; you are *sing. form.*

  siamo see-<u>ah</u>moh   we are
  esserci eh<u>s</u>-sehrchee   to give; to be present
  c'è/ci sono   there is; there are
  cheh/chee <u>soh</u>noh

Language Tip

C'è is used for a singular noun as in *Non c'è questa taglia* (We don't have this size). If the noun following is in the plural, you say: *Ci sono due letti* (There are two beds).

---

80 **avere** ah<u>veh</u>reh   to have
  ho oh   I have
  hai <u>ahee</u>   you have *sing. inform.*
  ha ah   he/she/it has; you have *sing. form.*

  abbiamo   we have
  ahb-bee<u>ah</u>moh
  avete ah<u>veh</u>teh   you have *pl.*
  hanno <u>ahn</u>-noh   they have

Language Tip

The perfect tense is formed with the conjugated auxiliary verbs *avere* (to have) and *essere* (to be). For information on the past tense, see chapters 1 and 2.

---

81 **avere bisogno di** — to need; to require
 ah_veh_reh bee_zoh_nyoh dee

  ho bisogno di — I need
  oh bee_zoh_nyoh dee

  abbiamo bisogno di — we need
  ahb-bee_ah_moh
  bee_zoh_nyoh dee

82 **volere** voh_leh_reh — to want

  voglio _voh_-lyoh — I want
  vuoi voo-_ohee_ — you want *sing. inform.*
  vuole voo-_ohleh_ — he/she/it wants; you want
  — *sing. form.*

  vogliamo voh-_lyah_moh — we want
  volete voh_leh_teh — you want *pl.*
  vorrei vohr-_ray_ — I would like to
  vorresti vohr-_reh_stee — you would like to
  — *sing. inform.*

  vorremmo — we would like to
  vohr-_rehm_-moh

83 **potere** poh_teh_reh — can; to be able to;
  — to be allowed to

  posso _pohs_-soh — I can
  può poo-_oh_ — he/she/it can; you can
  — *sing. form.*

  possiamo — we can
  pohs-see-_ah_moh
  potrebbe — he/she/it could; you could
  poh_trehb_-beh — *sing. form.*
  potuto poh_too_toh — been able/allowed to

84 **stare** <u>stah</u>reh — to stay; to remain; to be
   sto stoh — I stand/am
   stai <u>stah</u>-eeh — you stand/are
   sta stah — he/she/it stands/is
   — you stand/are *sing. form.*

   stiamo stee-<u>ah</u>moh — we stand/are
   state <u>stah</u>teh — you stand/are *pl.*
   stato <u>stah</u>toh — been

85 **fare** <u>fah</u>reh — to do; to make
   faccio <u>fah</u>tchoh — I make
   fa fah — he/she/it makes; you make *sing. form.*

   facciamo fah-tch<u>ah</u>moh — we make

   fate fateh — you make *pl.*
   fanno <u>fah</u>n-noh — they make
   fatto <u>fah</u>ttoh — made

86 **piacere** pee-ah<u>cheh</u>reh — to like; to enjoy
   piace pee-<u>ah</u>cheh — he/she/it likes; you like *sing. form.*

   il piacere eel pee-ah<u>cheh</u>reh — pleasure
   per piacere pehr pee-ah<u>cheh</u>reh — please

87 **andare** ahn<u>dah</u>reh — to go
   andarci ahn<u>dah</u>rchee — to go to
   vado <u>vah</u>doh — I go
   vai <u>vah</u>-ee — you go *sing. inform.*
   va vah — he/she/it goes; you go *sing. form.*

   andiamo ahndee-<u>ah</u>moh — we go

   andate ahn<u>dah</u>teh — you go *pl.*
   vanno <u>vah</u>n-noh — they go

88 **capire** kah<u>pee</u>reh — to understand
   capisco kah<u>pee</u>skoh — I understand
   capisci kah<u>pee</u>she — you understand *sing. inform.*
   capisce kah<u>pee</u>sheh — he/she/it understands; you understand *sing. form.*

   capito kah<u>pee</u>toh — understood

89 **vedere** veh<u>deh</u>reh — to see
   vedi <u>veh</u>dee — you see
   vede <u>veh</u>deh — he/she/it sees; you see *sing. form.*

   vediamo vehdee-<u>ah</u>moh — we see
   visto <u>vee</u>stoh — seen

90 **prendere** <u>prehn</u>-dehreh — to take
   prendo <u>prehn</u>doh — I take
   prende <u>prehn</u>deh — he/she/it takes; you take *sing. form.*

   prendiamo prehndee-<u>ah</u>moh — we take
   preso <u>preh</u>zoh — taken

91 **dire** <u>dee</u>reh — to say; to speak
   dico <u>dee</u>koh — I say
   dice <u>dee</u>cheh — he/she/it says; you say *sing. form.*

   detto <u>deht</u>-toh — said

92 **costare** koh<u>stah</u>reh — to cost
   costa <u>koh</u>stah — it costs
   costano <u>koh</u>stahnoh — they cost

93 **pagare** pah<u>gah</u>reh — to pay
   pago <u>pah</u>goh — I pay
   pagato pah<u>gah</u>toh — paid

94 **aiutare** ahyou-_tah_reh — to help
    aiuti ah_you_tee — you help *sing. inform.*
    aiuta ah_you_tah — he/she/it helps; you help *sing. form.*

    aiutate ahyou_tah_-teh — you help *pl.*
    aiutato ahyou_tah_-toh — helped
    l'aiuto ♂ lah_you_toh — help; assistance

95 **chiamare** key-ah_mah_reh — to call; to telephone
    chiamo key-_ah_moh — I call
    chiami key-_ah_mee — you call *sing. inform.* Call!

    chiama key-_ah_mah — he/she/it calls; you call *sing. form.*

    chiamate key-ah_mah_teh — you are called *pl.* Call!
    chiamato key-ah_mah_toh — called

    chiamarsi key-ah_mahr_see — to name
    mi chiamo me key-_ah_moh — I am called
    ti chiami tee key-_ah_mee — you are called *sing. inform.*
    si chiama see key-_ah_mah — he/she/it is called; you are called *sing. form.*
    vi chiamate vee key-ah_mah_teh — you are called *pl.*

96 **aprire** ah_pree_reh — to open
    apre ah_preh_ — he/she/it opens; you open *sing. form.*

    aprite ah_pree_teh — you open *pl.*
    aperto ah_pehr_toh — open

97	**mangiare** mahn<u>j</u>ahreh	to eat
	mangio mahn<u>j</u>oh	I eat
	mangi mahn<u>j</u>ee	you eat *sing. inform.*
	mangia mahn<u>j</u>ah	he/she/it eats; you eat *sing. form.*
	mangiato mahn<u>j</u>ahtoh	eaten
98	**bere** <u>be</u>hreh	to drink
	bevo <u>be</u>hvoh	I drink
	bevuto beh<u>voo</u>toh	drunk
99	**perdere** <u>pe</u>hrdehreh	to lose
	perdersi <u>pe</u>hrdehrsee	to lose one's way; to get lost
	perso <u>pe</u>hrsoh	
100	**trovare** troh<u>va</u>hreh	to find
	trovo <u>troh</u>voh	I find
	trova <u>troh</u>vah	he/she/it finds; you find *sing. form.*
	troviamo trohvee-<u>ah</u>moh	we find
	trovarsi troh<u>va</u>hrsee	to find (oneself)
	si trova see <u>troh</u>vah	he/she/it finds (him-/her-/itself)

Language Tip

Many Italian verbs end in *-are*. To conjugate the present tense of these verbs, replace the *-are* ending with *-o, -i, -a, -iamo, -ate, -ano* for the respective person: for example, *trovo* (I find), *trovi* (you find), *trova* (he/she/it finds; you *sing. form.* find), *troviamo* (we find), *trovate* (you *pl.* find), *trovano* (they find).

Verbs ending in *-ere* are conjugated in the present tense with the endings *-o, -i, -e, -iamo, -ete, -ono*. For example: *perdo* (I lose), *perdi* (you lose), *perde* (he/she/it loses; you *sing. form.* lose), *perdiamo* (we lose), *perdete* (you *pl.* lose), *perdono* (they lose).

Verbs ending in *-ire* are often conjugated irregularly.

Meeting People

Greetings

The following greeting can be used during the day, in the evening or at night. As it is informal, be careful to use it only with someone you are on familiar terms with:

Ciao! <u>chah</u>-oh   Hi!/Hello!

For a more formal greeting, you can say:

Buongiorno. bwohn-<u>john</u>noh   Good morning./Good day.

Buona sera. bwohnah <u>seh</u>rah   Good evening.

Country and Culture Tip

Young people in Italy generally use the informal address of *tu* and the salutation *ciao*, which is both a greeting and a farewell.

When you do not know someone, use the formal address of *lei* and the greetings *buongiorno* and *buona sera*. When parting use the polite *arrivederci*.

Italians commonly shake hands when greeting one another. Relatives and friends will often kiss on both cheeks, and the younger generation even extends this to three kisses.

If you want to show how pleased you are to see someone:

Che bello vederti!
keh <u>behl</u>-loh veh-<u>dehr</u>tee

How nice to see
you again! *sing. inform.*

Che bello vedervi!
keh <u>behl</u>-loh veh-<u>dehr</u>vee

How nice to see
you again! *pl.*

Che bello vederLa!
keh <u>behl</u>-loh veh-<u>dehr</u>lah

How nice to see
you! *sing. form.*

Language Tip

In Italian, *vedersi* means "seeing (meeting) one another".
The term is made up of the verb *vedere* (to see) and the pronoun *si* (oneself). In the pronunciation, the last *e* of the verb
is omitted. This also applies to other verbs such as: *capirsi*
(to understand one another), *aiutarsi* (to help one
another), *aprirsi* (to open up to one another).
Depending on the usage, *si* can be replaced by the appropriate pronoun: *vedermi* (seeing me), *vederti* (seeing you),
vederlo (seeing him), *vederla* (seeing one another), *vederLa*
(seeing them), *vederci* (seeing us), *vedervi* (seeing you *pl.*).

Saying Good-bye

If you want to say good-bye formally, say:

Arrivederci. ahr-reeveh-<u>dehr</u>chee   Good-bye.

ArrivederLa. ahr-reeveh-<u>dehr</u>lah   Good-bye. *sing. form.*

Buona notte. bwohnah <u>noht</u>-teh   Good night.

If you want to be more informal:

Ciao! <u>chah</u>-oh — Bye!/Ciao!

Ci si vede!* chee see <u>veh</u>deh — See you!

Ci vediamo. chee veh-dee-<u>ah</u>moh — We'll see each other.

If you want to be more specific when departing, say:

A più tardi! ah pew <u>tahr</u>dee — See you later!

Ciao, a più tardi!
<u>chah</u>-oh ah pew <u>tahr</u>dee — Bye, until later!

A stasera! ah stah-<u>seh</u>rah — Until tonight!

A domani! ah doh<u>mah</u>-nee — Until tomorrow!

A domani mattina!
ah doh<u>mah</u>-nee maht-<u>tee</u>nah — Until tomorrow morning!

A domani sera!
ah doh<u>mah</u>-nee <u>seh</u>rah — Until tomorrow evening!

Ci vediamo stasera.
chee veh-dee-<u>ah</u>moh
stah-<u>seh</u>rah — We'll see each other tonight.

Ci vediamo domani.
chee veh-dee-<u>ah</u>moh doh<u>mah</u>-nee — We'll see each other tomorrow.

Ci vediamo domani mattina.
chee veh-dee-<u>ah</u>moh doh<u>mah</u>-nee
maht-<u>tee</u>nah — We'll see each other tomorrow morning.

---

* Idiomatic expression:
  Ci si vede! chee see <u>veh</u>deh — See you!

Ci vediamo domani sera.
chee veh-dee-<u>ah</u>moh doh<u>mah</u>-nee <u>seh</u>rah

We'll see each other tomorrow evening.

Ci vediamo all'una.
chee veh-dee-<u>ah</u>moh ahl-<u>loo</u>nah

We'll see each other at one o'clock.

Language Tip

If the preposition *a* (to; at) precedes an article, the two will merge. For example: *a+il* becomes *al* (*al giorno* – "on the day"), *a+l'* becomes *all'* (*l'una* – *all'una*) and *a+le* becomes *alle* (*le due* – *alle due*).

Ci vediamo alle due.
chee veh-dee-<u>ah</u>moh <u>ahl</u>-leh <u>doo</u>-eh

We'll see each other at two o'clock.

Ci vediamo domani all'una.
chee veh-dee-<u>ah</u>moh doh<u>mah</u>-nee ahl-<u>loo</u>nah

We'll see each other tomorrow at one o'clock.

Ci vediamo domani alle due.
chee veh-dee-<u>ah</u>moh doh<u>mah</u>-nee <u>ahl</u>-leh <u>doo</u>-eh

We'll see each other tomorrow at two o'clock.

Ci vediamo alle ... [time].
chee veh-dee-<u>ah</u>moh <u>ahl</u>-leh

We'll see each other at ...

Ci vediamo domani alle ... [time]. chee veh-dee-<u>ah</u>moh doh<u>mah</u>-nee <u>ahl</u>-leh

We'll see each other tomorrow at ...

Ci vediamo alle ... [time] di mattina. chee veh-dee-<u>ah</u>moh <u>ahl</u>-leh ... dee maht-<u>tee</u>nah

We'll see each other at ... in the morning.

Ci vediamo alle ... [time] di sera. chee veh-dee-<u>ah</u>moh <u>ahl</u>-leh ... dee <u>seh</u>rah

We'll see each other at ... in the evening.

Language Tip

Italian uses the 12-hour clock, so when you are talking about times, specify if it's in the morning (*di mattina*) or afternoon (*di sera*), for example *le otto di sera* (eight o'clock at night).

Other important terms to know are *quarto* (quarter), *mezza* (half) and *meno* (less; minus).

Examples:

8:15	*le otto e un quarto*
8:25	*le otto e venticinque*
8:30	*le otto e mezza*
8:45	*le nove meno un quarto*

If you know on what day you'll see someone again:

Ci vediamo ...
chee veh-dee-<u>ah</u>moh

We'll see each other on ...

See page 111–112 for numbers and days of the week.

You can also specify where you'll meet again:

Ci vediamo …   We'll see each other in …
chee veh-dee-<u>ah</u>moh

all'hotel
ahl-loh<u>tehl</u>

al ristorante
ahl reestoh-<u>rahn</u>teh

al bar
ahl bahr

in piscina
een pee<u>sheen</u>ah

in spiaggia
en spee-<u>ahd</u>jah

al mercato
ahl mehr<u>kah</u>toh

in discoteca
een
deeskoh-<u>teh</u>kah

allo stadio
<u>ahl</u>-loh
<u>stah</u>dee-oh

To wish someone well when you depart, say:

Tante belle cose!*   All the best!
<u>tahn</u>teh <u>behl</u>-leh <u>koh</u>zeh

---

* Idiomatic expression:
  Tante belle cose! <u>tahn</u>teh <u>behl</u>-leh <u>koh</u>zeh   All the best!

Introductions

To introduce yourself or someone else, say:

Mi chiamo ... mee key-<u>ah</u>moh   My name is ...

Language Tip

Chiamarsi is the reflexive form of *chiamare* (to call; to telephone) and means "to name, to be called". In the conjugated form, the pronoun precedes the verb: *mi chiamo* (I'm called), *ti chiami* (you are called *sing. inform.*), *si chiama* (he/she/it is called), *vi chiamate* (you are called *pl .inform.*).

Sono ... <u>soh</u>noh   I am ...

Siamo ... [your name] e ... [name of your partner]. see-<u>ah</u>moh ... eh   We are ... and ...

Questo è ... [name] ♂.
<u>kweh</u>stoh eh   This is ...

Questa è ... [name] ♀.
<u>kweh</u>stah eh   This is ...

Questi sono Paolo ♂ e Paola ♀.
<u>kweh</u>stee <u>soh</u>noh <u>pah</u>-ohloh
eh <u>pah</u>-ohlah   This is Paolo and Paola.

Queste sono Anna ♀ e Maria ♀.
<u>kweh</u>steh <u>soh</u>noh <u>ahn</u>-nah eh
mah-<u>ree</u>-ah   This is Anna and Maria.

Language Tip

When talking about a group of people, the gender of the pronoun or the adjective follows the gender of the group. If the group is all men, the endings of pronouns and adjectives are masculine (e.g. *questi*). If the group is all women, the endings are feminine (e. g. *queste*). If, however, there are men and women in a group—and even if there is just one man among 200 women—the ending will be masculine.

When you are introduced to someone, you can say:

Piacere.* pee-ah<u>cheh</u>reh   My pleasure.

Piacere, sono ... [your name].   My pleasure. I am ...
pee-ah<u>cheh</u>reh <u>soh</u>noh

If you didn't get someone's name, just ask again:

Scusa, come ti chiami?   Excuse me, what is
<u>skoo</u>zah <u>koh</u>meh tee key-<u>ah</u>mee   your name? *sing. inform.*

Scusi, come si chiama?   Excuse me, what is
<u>skoo</u>zee <u>koh</u>me see key-<u>ah</u>mah   your name? *sing. form.*

Scusa, non ho capito il tuo   I'm sorry, I didn't get
nome. <u>skoo</u>zah nohn oh   your name. *sing. inform.*
kah<u>pee</u>toh eel <u>too</u>-oh <u>noh</u>meh

Scusi, non ho capito il suo   I'm sorry, I didn't
nome. <u>skoo</u>zee nohn oh   get your name. *sing. form.*
kah<u>pee</u>toh eel <u>soo</u>-oh <u>noh</u>meh

---

* Idiomatic expression:
  Piacere. pee-ah<u>cheh</u>reh   My pleasure.

Language Tip

One form of the past tense is constructed with the conjugations of the verb *avere* (to have) and participles such as *capito* (understood), *aiutato* (helped) and *pagato* (paid), e.g.

ho capito	I understood
hai aiutato	you've helped *sing. form.*
avete pagato	you've paid *pl.*

If you want to find out the name of the person you are talking to:

Come si chiama?
<u>koh</u>me see key-<u>ah</u>mah

What's your name?
sing. form.

Come ti chiami?
<u>koh</u>meh tee key-<u>ah</u>mee

What's your name?
sing. inform.

Come vi chiamate?
<u>koh</u>meh vee key-ah<u>mah</u>teh

What's your name? *pl.*

Qual'è il suo nome?
<u>kwah</u>leh eel <u>soo</u>-oh <u>noh</u>meh

What's your name? *sing.
form.*

Qual'è il tuo nome?
<u>kwah</u>leh eel <u>too</u>-oh <u>noh</u>meh

What's your name?
sing. inform.

Language Tip

The word *quale* is used in the expression *qual'è* (which is). For easier pronunciation the final *-e* of *quale* is dropped. In the plural, however, the *-i* of *quali* stays, as in: *Quali sono i miei biglietti?* (Which are my tickets?)

If you're traveling, you might encounter some unfamiliar names:

Che bel nome! keh behl <u>noh</u>meh — What a lovely name!

È un nome molto bello! eh oon <u>noh</u>meh <u>mohl</u>toh <u>behl</u>-loh — That is a lovely name!

Mi piace questo nome! mee pee-<u>ah</u>cheh <u>kwehs</u>toh <u>noh</u>meh — I like that name!

Mi piace molto questo nome! mee pee-<u>ah</u>cheh <u>mohl</u>toh <u>kwehs</u>toh <u>noh</u>meh — I like that name very much!

Che nome è? keh <u>noh</u>meh eh — What kind of a name is that?

Saying Thanks

Here are a number of ways to say thank you:

Grazie. <u>grah</u>tzee-eh — Thanks.

Grazie tanto! <u>grah</u>tzee-eh <u>tahn</u>toh — Many thanks!

Grazie di tutto! <u>grah</u>tzee-eh dee <u>toot</u>-toh — Thanks for everything.

Grazie per tutto questo. <u>grah</u>tzee-eh pehr <u>toot</u>-toh <u>kwehs</u>toh — Thanks for all that.

If you are thanked by someone else, you can respond with:

Non c'è di che.* nohn cheh dee keh — No problem./ You're welcome.

---

* Idiomatic expression:
   Non c'è di che. nohn cheh dee keh — No problem. / You're welcome.

Country and Culture Tip

Though it is not incorrect to say *prego* in reply to *grazie*, it is not particularly polite either. *Non c'è di che* for "You're welcome" is more appropriate.

Di niente! dee nee-<u>ehn</u>teh

Don't mention it!

Grazie a voi!
<u>grah</u>tzee-eh ah <u>voh</u>-ee

I thank you! *pl.*

If someone else has done something for you and you wish to thank them for it, say:

Grazie per il tuo aiuto.
<u>grah</u>tzee-eh pehr eel <u>too</u>-oh ah<u>you</u>toh

Thank you for your help.
sing. inform.

Grazie per il suo aiuto.
<u>grah</u>tzee-eh pehr eel <u>soo</u>-oh ah<u>you</u>toh

Thank you for your help.
sing. form.

Grazie per il vostro aiuto.
<u>grah</u>tzee-eh pehr eel <u>voh</u>stroh ah<u>you</u>toh

Thank you for your help.
pl.

Grazie che mi aiuti.
<u>grah</u>tzee-eh keh mee ah<u>you</u>tee

Thank you for helping me.
sing. inform.

Grazie che mi aiuta.
<u>grah</u>tzee-eh keh mee ah<u>you</u>tah

Thank you for helping me.
sing. form.

Grazie che mi aiutate.
<u>grah</u>tzee-eh keh mee ah<u>you</u>tahteh

Thank you for helping me.
pl.

Grazie per avere aiutato.
<u>grah</u>tzee-eh pehr ah<u>veh</u>reh ah<u>you</u>tahtoh

Thank you for your help.
sing. form.

Grazie per avere pagato.
grahtzee-eh pehr ahvehreh
pahgahtoh

Thanks for paying (the bill).

Grazie che hai pagato per me.
grahtzee-eh keh ahee pahgahtoh
pehr meh

Thank you for paying
for me. *sing. inform.*

Grazie che hai pagato per noi.
grahtzee-eh keh ahee pahgahtoh
pehr noh-ee

Thank you for paying for
us. *sing. inform.*

Grazie che avete pagato per noi.
grahtzee-eh keh ahvehteh
pahgahtoh pehr noh-eei

Thank you for paying
for us. *pl.*

Grazie per essere qui con noi.
grahtzee-eh pehr ehs-sehreh
kwee kohn noh-ee

Thank you for being
with us.

Grazie che sei qui con me.
grahtzee-eh keh say kwee
kohn meh

Thank you for being
with me. *sing. inform.*

Grazie che è qui con me.
grahtzee-eh keh eh kwee
kohn meh

Thank you for being
with me. *sing. form.*

**Grazie per avermi fatto questo
piacere.** grahtzee-eh pehr
ahvehrmee faht-toh kwehstoh
pee-ahchehreh

Thank you for helping me.
sing. form.

**Grazie per averci fatto questo
piacere.** grahtzee-eh pehr
ahvehrchee faht-toh kwehstoh
pee-ahchehreh

Thank you for helping us.
sing. form.

Language Tip

If a pronoun such as *mi, ti, si, vi, ci* or *lo, la, le* is combined with a verb in the infinitive, the pronoun is added to the end of the verb, and the *e* at the end of the verb is dropped.
lo capisco = I understand him, but
capirlo = to understand him
ti aiuto = I help you, but *aiutarti* = to help you

To thank someone for something specific:

Grazie per questo bel regalo!
grahtzee-eh pehr kwehstoh behl
rehgahloh

Thank you for this nice present!

Grazie tanto per questo bel regalo! grahtzee-eh tahntoh pehr kwehstoh behl rehgahloh

Thank you so much for this nice present!

Grazie per questa bella camera.
grahtzee-eh pehr kwehstah
behl-lah kahmehrah

Thank you for this nice room.

Grazie tanto per questa camera.
grahtzee-eh tahntoh pehr
kwehstah kahmehrah

Thank you so much for this room.

Grazie per questo pasto.
grahtzee-eh pehr kwehstoh
pahstoh

Thank you for this meal.

Grazie tanto per questo pasto.
grahtzee-eh tahntoh pehr
kwehstoh pahstoh

Thank you so much for this meal.

Grazie per questo buon ... Thank you for the good ...
grahtzee-eh pehr kwehstoh bwohn

caffè **vino** **tè** **aperitivo**
kahf-feh vee-noh teh ah-pehree-teevoh

Grazie per questa buona ... Thank you for the good ...
grahtzee-eh pehr kwehstah bwohnah

birra **pasta** **limonata** **marmellata**
beer-rah pahstah leemohnahtah mahrmehl-lahtah

Communication Difficulties

If you find it difficult to understand what is being said, just ask:

Scusi? skoozee Excuse me? *sing. form.*

If you are on familiar terms with someone, you could use the informal:

Scusa? skoozah Excuse me? *sing. inform.*

Or if you are addressing a group of people:

Scusate? skoo<u>zah</u>teh   Excuse me? *pl.*

But always:

Come? <u>koh</u>meh   Excuse me?/
                                          What was that again?

Cosa? <u>koh</u>zah   What (was that)?

Or more detailed:

Non ho capito.   I didn't understand this.
nohn oh kah<u>pee</u>toh

Non ho capito bene.   I didn't exactly understand
nohn oh kah<u>pee</u>toh <u>beh</u>neh   this.

If they lost you completely, just say:

Scusi, non capisco.   I'm sorry, I don't
<u>skoo</u>zee nohn kah<u>pee</u>skoh   understand.

Scusa, non ti capisco.   I'm sorry, I don't
<u>skoo</u>zah nohn tee kah<u>pee</u>skoh   understand you.
                                          sing. inform.

Scusi, non la capisco.   I'm sorry, I don't
<u>skoo</u>zee nohn lah kah<u>pee</u>skoh   understand you. *sing. form.*

Non ti capisco più.   I don't understand you
nohn tee kah<u>pee</u>skoh pew   anymore. *sing. inform.*

Ora non ti capisco più.   Now you lost me.
<u>oh</u>rah nohn tee kah<u>pee</u>skoh pew   *sing. inform.*

Non La capisco più.
nohn lah kah<u>pee</u>skoh pew

I don't understand
you anymore. *sing. form.*

Ora non La capisco più.
<u>oh</u>rah nohn lah kah<u>pee</u>skoh pew

Now I don't understand
you at all. *sing. form.*

Non capisco più niente.
nohn kah<u>pee</u>skoh pew nee-<u>ehn</u>teh

I don't understand
anything at all.

Ora non capisco più niente.
<u>oh</u>rah nohn kah<u>pee</u>skoh pew
nee-<u>ehn</u>teh

Now you lost me
completely.

Language Tip

The simplest form of negation is *non,* which means "not".
Other options to negate a sentence are:

non … più	no more
non … niente	nothing
non … più niente	nothing anymore
non … per niente	not at all
non … ancora	not yet

Keep in mind that *non* is followed by the conjugated verb:
Non voglio più.   I don't want anymore.

If you don't know the word for a specific object, you may want to
point at it and ask:

Come si chiama questo?
<u>koh</u>meh see key-<u>ah</u>mah <u>kweh</u>stoh

What is this called?

Come si chiama questa cosa?
<u>koh</u>meh see key-<u>ah</u>mah
<u>kweh</u>stah <u>koh</u>zah

What do you call this?

Cos'è questo?   What's that?
koh<u>zeh</u> <u>kweh</u>stoh

If you are not sure whether the word you used was correct, point at the object in question and ask:

Non è un … ♂   Isn't that a …?
[repeat the word]?
nohn eh oon

Non è una … ♀   Isn't that a …?
[repeat the word]?
nohn eh <u>oo</u>nah

Non si può dire?   Can't you say that?
nohn see <u>poo</u>-oh <u>dee</u>reh

Non si dice?   Don't you say that?
nohn see <u>dee</u>cheh

To confirm that you have been understood correctly, say:

Mi capisci? mee kah<u>pee</u>shee   Do you understand me?
sing. inform.

Mi capisce? mee kah<u>pee</u>sheh   Do you understand me?
sing. form.

Mi faccio capire*?   Am I making myself clear?
mee <u>fah</u>tchoh kah<u>pee</u>reh

---

* Idiomatic expression:
   Mi faccio capire? mee <u>fah</u>tchoh kah<u>pee</u>reh   Am I making myself clear?

Capisci quello che dico?
kahpeeshee kwehl-loh keh deekoh

Do you understand what I'm saying? *sing. inform.*

Capisce quello che dico?
kahpeesheh kwehl-loh keh deekoh

Do you understand what I'm saying? *sing. form.*

Si capisce quello che dico?
see kahpeesheh kwehl-loh keh deekoh

Is what I'm saying understandable?

Hai capito? ahee kahpeetoh

Did you understand? *sing. inform.*

Ha capito? ah kahpeetoh

Did you understand? *sing. form.*

Avete capito? ahvehteh kahpeetoh

Did you understand? *pl.*

Small Talk

Health

It is common to ask about people's well-being, even if you do not expect a lengthy answer.

Come stai? <u>koh</u>meh <u>stah</u>-ee   How are you? *sing. inform.*

Come sta? <u>koh</u>meh stah   How are you? *sing. form.*

Come state? <u>koh</u>meh <u>stah</u>-teh   How are you? *pl.*

> ### Language Tip
> In spoken language, Italians use only one verb form for "you" in the plural. The expression *Come state?* (How are you?), therefore, can be used when addressing friends, family and strangers.

Come stai oggi?
<u>koh</u>meh <u>stah</u>-ee <u>oh</u>djee

How are you today?
sing. inform.

Come sta oggi?
<u>koh</u>meh stah <u>oh</u>djee

How are you today?
sing. form.

Come state oggi?
<u>koh</u>meh <u>stah</u>-the <u>oh</u>djee

How are you today?
pl.

If you want it to sound more relaxed, simply say:

Come va? <u>koh</u>meh vah   How are you? (What's up?)

Come vanno le cose?   How's it going?
<u>koh</u>meh <u>vahn</u>-noh leh <u>koh</u>zeh

Ciao, come va?   Hi, how are you?
<u>chah</u>-oh <u>koh</u>meh vah

If someone hasn't been feeling well lately, you could say:

Stai meglio? <u>stah</u>-ee <u>meh</u>lyoh — Are you feeling any better? *sing. inform.*

Stai meglio ora?
<u>stah</u>-ee <u>meh</u>lyoh <u>oh</u>rah — Are you any better now? *sing. inform.*

Stai meglio oggi?
<u>stah</u>-ee <u>meh</u>lyoh <u>oh</u>djee — Are you any better today? *sing. inform.*

Sta meglio? stah <u>meh</u>lyoh — Are you feeling any better? *sing. form.*

Sta meglio ora?
stah <u>meh</u>lyoh <u>oh</u>rah — Are you any better now? *sing. form.*

Sta meglio oggi?
stah <u>meh</u>lyoh <u>oh</u>djee — Are you any better today? *sing. form.*

Va meglio ora?
vah <u>meh</u>lyoh <u>oh</u>rah — Is it better now?

Va meglio oggi?
vah <u>meh</u>lyoh <u>oh</u>djee — Is it better today?

Hopefully the answer will be:

Bene. <u>beh</u>neh — Good.

Molto bene. <u>mohl</u>toh <u>beh</u>neh — Very good.

Bene, grazie. <u>beh</u>neh <u>grah</u>tzee-eh — Good, thanks.

Molto bene, grazie.
<u>mohl</u>toh <u>beh</u>neh <u>grah</u>tzee-eh — Very good, thanks.

Sto molto bene, grazie.
stoh <u>mohl</u>toh <u>beh</u>neh <u>grah</u>tzee-eh — I'm doing very well, thanks.

E voi? eh <u>voh</u>-ee — And what about you? *pl.*

Stiamo bene, grazie.
stee-ahmoh behneh grahtzee-eh

We are fine, thanks.

Stiamo molto bene, grazie.
stee-ahmoh mohltoh behneh
grahtzee-eh

We are doing very well, thanks.

Meglio, grazie. mehlyoh
grahtzee-eh

Better, thanks.

Molto meglio, grazie.
mohltoh mehlyoh grahtzee-eh

Much better, thanks.

Sto meglio, grazie.
stoh mehlyoh grahtzee-eh

I'm better, thanks.

Stiamo meglio, grazie.
stee-ahmoh mehlyoh grahtzee-eh

We're better, thanks.

Sto meglio oggi. stoh
mehlyoh ohdjee

I'm better today.

Stiamo meglio oggi.
stee-ahmoh mehlyoh ohdjee

We're better today.

The answer may be less positive:

Non tanto bene.
nohn tahntoh behneh

Not very well.

Non sto tanto bene.
nohn stoh tahntoh behneh

I'm not too well.

Non stiamo tanto bene.
nohn stee-ahmoh tahntoh behneh

We're not too well.

Male. mahleh

Badly.

Sto male. stoh mahleh

I'm feeling badly.

Oggi sto male. <u>oh</u>djee
stoh <u>mah</u>leh

I'm feeling badly today.

Mi sono rotto ... ♂.
me <u>soh</u>no <u>roht</u>-toh

I broke my ...

Mi sono rotta ... ♀.
me <u>soh</u>no <u>roht</u>-tah

I broke my ...

la gamba
lah <u>gahm</u>bah

il braccio
eel <u>brah</u>-tchoh

la mano
lah <u>mah</u>noh

il piede
eel pee-
<u>eh</u>deh

Language Tip

To form the past tense in Italian, use the auxiliary verbs
avere (to have) and *essere* (to be). Verbs that form their past
tense with *essere* (to be) will change the participle to agree
with the person or thing they relate to:
sono andata ♀ (I went), *sei andato* ♂ (you went),
siamo andati ♂ (we went), *sono andate* ♀ (they went).
The endings of the participles correspond to the endings of
pronouns and adjectives: *-a* and *-e* for the feminine, and *-o*
and *-i* for the masculine.

Background

One of the first questions usually asked is where someone comes from. To ask or answer this, you could say:

Di dove sei? dee <u>doh</u>veh say

Where are you from?
sing. inform.

Di dov'è? dee doh<u>veh</u>

Where are you from?
sing. form.

Sono dalla Stati Uniti d'America*. I'm from the USA.
<u>soh</u>noh <u>dehl</u>-lah <u>stah</u>tee oo<u>nee</u>tee
dah<u>meh</u>-reekah

Siamo dalla Stati Uniti d'America*. We're from the USA.
see-<u>ah</u>moh <u>dehl</u>-lah <u>stah</u>tee
oo<u>nee</u>tee dah<u>meh</u>-reekah

> ### Language Tip
>
> If the word *da* (to; from; since) comes before a noun, the two words merge. Thus, *da + la* become *dalla* (*dalla Stati Uniti d'America* – from the United States of America) and *da + l'* becomes *dall'* (*dall'Inghilterra* – from England).

E dove in ... [country]?
eh <u>doh</u>veh een

And where in ...?

Sono di ... [city].
<u>soh</u>noh dee

I'm from ...

Siamo di ... [city].
see-<u>ah</u>moh dee

We're from ...

---

* **Gran-Bretagna** grahn breh<u>tah</u>nyah

Great Britain

Canada kah-nah-<u>dah</u>

Canada

È vicino a … [city].
eh vee<u>chee</u>noh ah

It is close to …

È molto vicino a … [city].
eh <u>mohl</u>toh vee<u>chee</u>noh ah

It is very close to …

Non è vicino a … [city]?
nohn eh vee<u>chee</u>noh ah

Isn't that close to …?

Sì, è vicino a … [city].
see eh vee<u>chee</u>noh ah

Yes, it is close to …

Sì, è molto vicino a … [city].
see eh <u>mohl</u>toh vee<u>chee</u>noh ah

Yes, it's very close to …

… [city] è molto vicina.
eh <u>mohl</u>toh vee<u>chee</u>nah

… is nearby.

Language Tip

In Italian, most city names are feminine. "New York is beautiful" is translated *New York è bella*.

Maybe the person you're talking to is from a city you've visited:

Oh, ci sono stato ♂!
oh chee <u>soh</u>noh <u>stah</u>toh

Oh, I've been there!

Oh, ci sono stata ♀!
oh chee <u>soh</u>noh <u>stah</u>tah

Oh, I've been there!

Oh, ci vado domani!
oh chee <u>vah</u>doh doh<u>mah</u>-nee

Oh, I'm going there tomorrow!

Oh, ci voglio andare domani!
oh chee <u>voh</u>-lyoh ahn<u>dah</u>reh doh<u>mah</u>-nee

Oh, that's where I want to go tomorrow!

Vorrei andarci!
vohr-<u>ray</u> ahn<u>dahr</u>chee

I'd like to go there
some time!

A … [city] è molto buono il …
ah …eh <u>mohl</u>toh <u>bwoh</u>noh eel

… has very good …

caffè
kahf-<u>feh</u>

formaggio
fohr<u>mah</u>djoh

cioccolato
chohk-koh<u>lah</u>toh

vino
<u>vee</u>-noh

A … [city] è molto buona la …
ah …eh <u>mohl</u>toh <u>bwoh</u>nah lah

… has very good …

pasta
<u>pah</u>stah

carne
<u>kahr</u>neh

pizza
<u>pee</u>-tzah

birra
<u>beer</u>-rah

Do You Like It Here?

You may want to tell others how much you enjoy a particular
thing or place, or you want to ask others for their impressions.
You could say:

Ti piace qui?
tee pee-<u>ah</u>cheh kwee

Do you like it here?
sing. inform.

Le piace qui?
leh pee-<u>ah</u>cheh kwee

Do you like it here?
sing. form.

Vi piace qui?
vee pee-<u>ah</u>cheh kwee

Do you like it here? *pl.*

Sì, molto. see <u>moh</u>ltoh

Yes, very much.

Sì, mi piace molto.
see me pee-<u>ah</u>cheh <u>moh</u>ltoh

Yes, I like it very much.

Sì, ci piace molto.
see chee pee-<u>ah</u>cheh <u>moh</u>ltoh

Yes, we like it very much.

Sì, è bello qui. see eh
<u>behl</u>-loh kwee

Yes, it is nice here.

Sì, è molto bello qui.
see eh <u>moh</u>ltoh <u>behl</u>-loh kwee

Yes, it is very nice here.

La camera è molto bella.
lah <u>kah</u>mehrah eh <u>moh</u>ltoh <u>behl</u>-lah

The room is very nice.

La ... è molto buona qui.
lah ... eh <u>moh</u>ltoh <u>bwoh</u>nah kwee

The ... is very good
here.

colazione
kohlatzee-<u>oh</u>neh

cena
<u>cheh</u>-nah

spiaggia
spee-<u>ah</u>djah

Il ... è molto buono qui.
eel ... eh <u>moh</u>ltoh <u>bwoh</u>noh kwee

The ... is very good
here.

servizio
sehr<u>vee</u>tzee-oh

pranzo
<u>prahn</u>tzoh

supermercato
soopehr-mehr<u>kah</u>toh

48

Or perhaps you prefer something else:

Non ti piace qui?
nohn tee pee-<u>ah</u>cheh kwee

Don't you like it here?
sing. inform.

Non le piace qui?
nohn leh pee-<u>ah</u>cheh kwee

Don't you like it here?
sing. form.

Non vi piace qui?
nohn vee pee-<u>ah</u>cheh kwee

Don't you like it here?
pl.

No, non mi piace tanto.
noh nohn me pee-<u>ah</u>cheh <u>tahn</u>toh

No, I don't like it much.

No, non ci piace.
noh nohn chee pee-<u>ah</u>cheh

No, we don't like it.

Non ci piace per niente qui.
nohn chee pee-<u>ah</u>cheh pehr nee-<u>ehn</u>teh kwee

We don't like it here at all.

Language Tip

The combination *non … per niente* (literally: not … for nothing) is translated into English as "not at all".

È stato più bello a …
[name of place]. eh <u>stah</u>toh pew <u>behl</u>-loh ah

It was nicer in …

È stato molto più bello a …
[name of place]. eh <u>stah</u>toh <u>mohl</u>toh pew <u>behl</u>-loh ah

It was much nicer in …

A … [name of place] è stata più bella la camera. ah … eh <u>stah</u>toh pew <u>behl</u>-lah lah <u>kah</u>mehrah

The room was nicer in …

A … [name of place] è stata più bella la … ah … eh <u>stah</u>toh pew <u>behl</u>-lah lah

The … was nicer in …

piscina
pee<u>she</u>-nah

vista
<u>vee</u>stah

spiaggia
spee-<u>ah</u>djah

A … [name of place] è stato più bello il letto. ah … eh <u>stah</u>toh pew <u>behl</u>-loh eel <u>leht</u>-toh

The bed in … was nicer.

A … [name of place] è stato più bello il … ah … ehrah pew <u>behl</u>-loh eel

The … in … was nicer.

bar
bahr

mare
<u>mah</u>reh

campeggio
kahm<u>peh</u>djoh

È stato più bello qui nel … [year]. eh <u>stah</u>toh pew <u>behl</u>-loh kwee nehl

In … it was nicer here.

Language Tip

Dates and years are read just like any other number. 1997 is *millenovecento-novantasette* (one thousand-nine hundred-ninety-seven). 2006 is formed according to the same pattern: *duemilasei*. Every year is preceded by the word *nel*, which is formed from the preposition *in* (in) and the article *il*.

Talking About Vacation Activities

To talk about what you like doing during your vacation, try these phrases:

Vado a letto tardi.
vahdoh ah <u>leht</u>-toh <u>tahr</u>dee

I go to bed late.

Noi andiamo a letto tardi.
<u>noh</u>-ee ahndee-<u>ah</u>moh ah <u>leht</u>-toh <u>tahr</u>dee

We go to bed late.

Vai a letto tardi?
<u>vah</u>-ee ah <u>leht</u>-toh <u>tahr</u>dee

Do you go to bed late?
sing. inform.

Vai a letto tardi!
<u>vah</u>-ee ah <u>leht</u>-toh <u>tahr</u>dee

You go to bed late!
sing. inform.

Voi due andate a letto tardi?
<u>voh</u>-ee <u>doo</u>-eh ahn<u>dah</u>teh ah <u>leht</u>-toh <u>tahr</u>dee

Do you two go to bed late? *pl.*

Voi due andate a letto tardi!
<u>voh</u>-ee doo-eh ahn<u>dah</u>teh ah <u>leht</u>-toh <u>tahr</u>dee

You two go to bed late! *pl.*

Language Tip

In Italian, the sentence constructions of questions do not differ from statements except in the way they are pronounced.

Non vado a letto tardi.
nohn <u>vah</u>doh ah <u>leht</u>-toh <u>tahr</u>dee

I don't go to bed late.

Non andiamo a letto tardi.
nohn ahndee-<u>ah</u>moh ah <u>leht</u>-toh <u>tahr</u>dee

We don't go to bed late.

Siamo … tutte le sere.
see-<u>ah</u>moh … <u>toot</u>-teh leh <u>seh</u>reh

We go to the …
every night.

in discoteca
een deeskoh
-<u>teh</u>kah

al bar
ahl bahr

al cinema
ahl <u>chee</u>nehmah

al casinò
ahl kahzee<u>noh</u>

Non voglio perdere tempo.
nohn <u>voh</u>-lyoh <u>pehr</u>dehreh <u>tehm</u>poh

I don't want to waste any time.

Non vogliamo perdere tempo.
nohn voh-<u>lyah</u>moh <u>pehr</u>dehreh <u>tehm</u>poh

We don't want to waste any time.

If you just need to relax, say:

Ho bisogno di tempo per me.
oh bee<u>zoh</u>nyoh dee <u>tehm</u>poh pehr meh

I need some time for myself.

Abbiamo bisogno di tempo per noi. ahb-beea<u>ah</u>moh bee<u>zoh</u>nyoh dee <u>tehm</u>poh pehr <u>noh</u>-ee

We need some time for ourselves.

To talk about how long you're staying:

Quanti giorni stai?
<u>kwahn</u>tee <u>johr</u>nee <u>stah</u>-ee

How many days are you
here? *sing. inform.*

Quanti giorni sta?
<u>kwahn</u>tee <u>johr</u>nee stah

How many days are
you here? *sing. form.*

Quanti giorni state?
<u>kwahn</u>tee <u>johr</u>nee <u>stah</u>-teh

How many days are
you here? *pl.*

**Siamo qui per … [number]
giorni – e voi?** see-<u>ah</u>moh kwee
pehr … <u>johr</u>nee eh <u>voh</u>-ee

We're here for … days,
and you? *pl.*

Da quanto tempo è qui?
dah <u>kwahn</u>toh <u>tehm</u>poh eh kwee

How long have you been
here already? *sing. inform.*

Da quanto tempo sei qui?
dah <u>kwahn</u>toh <u>tehm</u>poh say kwee

How long have you been
here already? *sing. form.*

**Sono qui da … [number]
giorni.**
<u>soh</u>noh kwee dah … <u>johr</u>nee

I have been here for ...
days.

**Siamo qui da … [number]
giorni – e voi?** see-<u>ah</u>moh kwee
dah … <u>johr</u>nee eh <u>voh</u>-ee

We have been here for ...
days, and you? *pl.*

See page 111 for numbers.

Weather

The weather is always a popular and easy conversation topic:

Che bel tempo!
keh behl <u>tehm</u>poh

What lovely weather!

Che bel tempo oggi!
keh behl <u>tehm</u>poh <u>oh</u>djee

What lovely weather today!

Fa bel tempo.
fah behl <u>tehm</u>poh

The weather is nice.

Fa bel tempo oggi.
fah behl <u>tehm</u>poh <u>oh</u>djee

The weather is nice today.

Sì, un tempo bellissimo!
see oon <u>tehm</u>poh behl-<u>lees</u>-seemoh

Yes, it's wonderful weather!

Che tempo fa? keh <u>tehm</u>poh fah

How's the weather?

Che tempo fa oggi?
keh <u>tehm</u>poh fah <u>oh</u>djee

How's the weather today?

Che bel tempo ieri!
keh behl <u>tehm</u>poh ee-<u>eh</u>ree

What wonderful weather we had yesterday!

Non abbiamo tanti giorni come questi in … [country].
nohn ahb-beeahmoh <u>tahn</u>tee <u>john</u>ree <u>koh</u>meh <u>kweh</u>stee een

We don't get many days like this in …

But even in Italy, there are days when the weather is not so great:

Fa brutto tempo.
fa <u>broot</u>-to <u>tehm</u>po

The weather is bad.

Fa brutto tempo oggi.
fah <u>broot</u>-toh <u>tehm</u>poh ohdjee

The weather is bad today.

Che brutto tempo oggi!
keh <u>broot</u>-toh <u>tehm</u>poh ohdjee

What horrible weather today!

Che brutto tempo ieri!
keh <u>broot</u>-toh <u>tehm</u>poh ee-<u>eh</u>ree

We had horrible weather yesterday!

Abbiamo tanti giorni come questi in … [country].
ahb-bee<u>ah</u>moh <u>tahn</u>tee <u>johr</u>nee <u>koh</u>meh <u>kweh</u>stee een

We get many days like that in …

C'è troppo … per me.
cheh <u>trohp</u>-poh … pehr meh

That's too much … for me.

C'è troppa … per noi.
cheh <u>trohp</u>-pah … pehr <u>noh</u>-ee

That's too much … for us.

Vorrei più … vohr-<u>ray</u> pew

I'd like more …

sole
<u>soh</u>-leh

pioggia
pee<u>oh</u>-djah

Or, if you like the weather just the way it is:

Per me va bene questo tempo!
pehr meh vah <u>beh</u>neh <u>kweh</u>stoh <u>tehm</u>poh

This weather is fine for me!

Per noi va bene questo tempo!
pehr <u>noh</u>-ee vah <u>beh</u>neh <u>kweh</u>stoh <u>teh</u>mpoh

This weather is fine for us!

A me piace questo tempo!
ah meh pee-<u>ah</u>cheh <u>kweh</u>stoh <u>teh</u>mpoh

I like this weather!

A noi piace questo tempo!
ah <u>noh</u>-ee pee-<u>ah</u>cheh <u>kweh</u>stoh <u>teh</u>mpoh

We like this weather!

Paying Compliments

Everyone likes a compliment. This is how you say it in Italian:

Questa cosa le sta molto bene. <u>kweh</u>stah <u>koh</u>zah leh stah <u>moh</u>ltoh <u>beh</u>neh

That looks great on you. *sing. form.*

Questa ... le sta molto bene. <u>kweh</u>stah ... leh stah <u>moh</u>ltoh <u>beh</u>neh

That ... looks great on you. *sing. form.*

camicia
kah<u>mee</u>chah

gonna
<u>gohn</u>-nah

cravatta
krah<u>vaht</u>-tah

giacca
<u>jahk</u>-kah

Questo ... le sta molto bene. <u>kweh</u>stoh ... leh stah <u>mohl</u>toh <u>beh</u>neh

That ... looks great on you. *sing. form.*

vestito
veh<u>stee</u>toh

pullover
pool-<u>loh</u>vehr

cappello
kahp-<u>pehl</u>-loh

costume
koh<u>stoo</u>meh

Language Tip

If you don't know the name for something don't be afraid to just call it a *cosa* (thing). You could also point at the object in question and ask for its name. This way you will easily expand your vocabulary.

The adjective *bello* can be used to compliment almost anything:

Che bello! keh <u>behl</u>-loh

How nice!

Che bella cosa!
keh <u>behl</u>-lah <u>koh</u>zah

What a lovely thing!

Che bella camera!
keh <u>behl</u>-lah <u>kah</u>mehrah

What a nice room!

Che bella ...! keh <u>behl</u>-lah

What a nice ...!

spiaggia
spee-<u>ahd</u>jah

chiesa
key-<u>ehz</u>ah

moto
<u>moh</u>toh

gonna
<u>gohn</u>-nah

Che bel nome! keh <u>behl</u> <u>noh</u>meh

What a lovely name!

Che bel ...! keh <u>behl</u>

What a lovely ...!

vestito
veh<u>stee</u>toh

cane
<u>kah</u>neh

gatto
<u>gaht</u>-toh

film
feelm

The word *buono* is used just as frequently:

I pasti sono buoni.
ee <u>pah</u>stee <u>soh</u>noh <u>bwoh</u>nee

The meals are good.

I pasti sono molto buoni.
ee <u>pah</u>stee <u>soh</u>noh <u>mohl</u>toh
<u>bwoh</u>nee

The meals are very good.

Questo letto è molto buono.
<u>kweh</u>stoh <u>leht</u>-toh eh <u>mohl</u>toh
<u>bwoh</u>noh

This bed is very good.

Questo ... è molto buono.
<u>kweh</u>stoh ... eh <u>mohl</u>toh <u>bwoh</u>noh

This ... is very good.

albergo
ahl<u>behr</u>goh

casco
<u>kah</u>skoh

ristorante
reestoh-<u>rah</u>nteh

vino
<u>vee</u>-noh

Questa ... è molto buona.
<u>kweh</u>stah ... eh <u>mohl</u>toh <u>bwoh</u>nah

This ... is very good.

pizza
<u>pee</u>-tzah

torta
<u>tohr</u>tah

tenda
<u>tehn</u>dah

pasta
<u>pah</u>stah

Accommodations
Finding a Room

If you are looking for an available room, say:

Ho bisogno di una camera.
oh bee<u>zoh</u>nyoh dee <u>oo</u>nah
<u>kah</u>mehrah

I need a room.

Abbiamo bisogno di una camera.
ahb-bee<u>ah</u>moh bee<u>zoh</u>nyoh
dee <u>oo</u>nah <u>kah</u>mehrah

We need a room.

Vorrei una camera.
vohr-<u>ray</u> <u>oo</u>nah <u>kah</u>mehrah

I would like a room.

Vorremmo una camera.
vohr-<u>rehm</u>-moh <u>oo</u>nah <u>kah</u>mehrah

We would like a room.

Vorrei una camera qui vicino.
vohr-<u>ray</u> <u>oo</u>nah <u>kah</u>mehrah
kwee vee<u>chee</u>noh

I would like a room
here in the area.

**Vorremmo una camera qui
vicino.** vohr-<u>rehm</u>-moh
<u>oo</u>nah <u>kah</u>mehrah kwee
vee<u>chee</u>noh

We would like a room
here in the area.

C'è un ... qui vicino?
cheh oon... kwee vee<u>chee</u>noh

Is there a ... nearby?

ufficio informazioni turistiche
oof-<u>fee</u>choh eenfohr-mahtzee-<u>oh</u>nee too<u>ree</u>stee-keh

Dove si trova? <u>doh</u>veh see <u>troh</u>vah — Where is it?

Ci può dire dove si trova? chee poo-<u>oh</u> <u>dee</u>reh <u>doh</u>veh see <u>troh</u>vah — Can you tell us where to find it? *sing. form.*

Mi può dire dove si trova? mee poo-<u>oh</u> <u>dee</u>reh <u>doh</u>veh see <u>troh</u>vah — Can you tell me where to find it? *sing. form.*

Come lo trovo? <u>koh</u>meh loh <u>troh</u>voh — How can I find it?

Come lo troviamo? <u>koh</u>meh loh trohvee-<u>ah</u>moh — How can we find it?

A che ora apre? a keh <u>oh</u>rah <u>ah</u>preh — What time does it open?

È aperto ora? eh ah<u>peh</u>rtoh <u>oh</u>rah — Is it open now?

Non è aperto ora? nohn eh ah<u>peh</u>rtoh <u>oh</u>rah — Isn't it open now?

È aperto domani? eh ah<u>peh</u>rtoh doh<u>mah</u>-nee — Is it open tomorrow?

Non è aperto domani? nohn eh ah<u>peh</u>rtoh doh<u>mah</u>-nee — Won't it be open tomorrow?

Grazie tanto per il suo aiuto. <u>grah</u>tzee-eh <u>tahn</u>toh pehr eel <u>soo</u>-oh ah<u>you</u>toh — Thank you very much for your help.

Once you've reached the tourist information office you can ask:

C'è ... qui vicino? chee... kwee vee<u>chee</u>noh — Is there a ... nearby?

un hotel oon oh<u>tehl</u>

un albergo oon ahl<u>behr</u>goh

una pensione oonah pehnsee-<u>oh</u>neh

Dov'è il … più vicino?
dohveh eel … pew veecheenoh

Where is the nearest …?

campeggio
kahmpehdjoh

Avete una …? ahvehteh oonah

Do you have a …?

carta stradale
kahrtah strahdahleh

carta geografica
kahrtah jehoh-grahfeekah

La posso avere?
lah pohs-soh ahvehreh

Can I have it?

La possiamo avere?
lah pohs-see-ahmoh ahvehreh

Can we have it?

Quanto costa? kwahntoh kohstah

How much does it cost?

To make sure you're getting a room within your price range, say:

Vorremmo una camera non troppo cara. vohr-rehm-moh oonahkahmehrah nohn trohp-poh kahrah

We'd like a room that is not too expensive.

Vorrei una camera non troppo cara. vohr-ray oonah kahmehrah nohn trohp-poh kahrah

I'd like a room that is not too expensive.

**Non posso pagare più di …
per una notte.** nohn <u>pohs</u>-soh
pah<u>gah</u>reh pew dee … pehr <u>oo</u>nah
<u>noht</u>-teh

I cannot pay more than …
per night.

**Non voglio pagare più di …
per una notte.** nohn <u>voh</u>-lyoh
pah<u>gah</u>reh pew dee … pehr <u>oo</u>nah
<u>noht</u>-teh

I don't want to pay more
than … per night.

See page 111 for numbers.

**Non possiamo pagare di più
per una notte.** nohn
pohs-see-<u>ah</u>moh pah<u>gah</u>reh
dee pew pehr <u>oo</u>nah <u>noht</u>-teh

We cannot pay more
for one night.

**Non vogliamo pagare di più
per una notte.** nohn voh-<u>lyah</u>moh
pah<u>gah</u>reh dee pew pehr <u>oo</u>nah
<u>noht</u>-teh

We don't want to spend
more for one night.

**Non voglio pagare tanto per
una camera.** nohn <u>voh</u>-lyoh
pah<u>gah</u>reh <u>tahn</u>toh pehr <u>oo</u>nah
<u>kah</u>mehrah

I don't want to pay that
much for a room.

**Non posso pagare tanto per
una camera.** nohn <u>pohs</u>-soh
pah<u>gah</u>reh <u>tahn</u>toh pehr <u>oo</u>nah
<u>kah</u>mehrah

I can't pay that much for
a room.

At the Reception

If you have booked a room in advance:

Avete una camera per me.
ah*veh*teh <u>oo</u>nah <u>kah</u>mehrah
pehr meh

You have a room for me.
sing. form.

Avete una camera per noi.
ah*veh*teh <u>oo</u>nah <u>kah</u>mehrah
pehr <u>noh</u>-ee

You have a room for us.
sing. form.

È per … [your name]. eh pehr

It is for …

Quale camera ho?
<u>kwah</u>leh <u>kah</u>mehrah oh

Which room do I have?

Quale camera abbiamo?
<u>kwah</u>leh <u>kah</u>mehrah ahb-bee<u>ah</u>moh

Which room do we have?

In case you don't have reservations, be more specific:

**Vorremmo una camera con
un letto.** ohr-<u>rehm</u>-moh <u>oo</u>nah
<u>kah</u>mehrah kohn oon <u>leht</u>-toh

We would like a room with
one bed.

**Abbiamo bisogno di un letto
grande.** ahb-bee<u>ah</u>moh bee-
<u>zoh</u>nyoh dee oon <u>leht</u>-toh <u>grahn</u>deh

We need a large bed.

**Prendiamo una camera con
due letti.** prehn-dee-<u>ah</u>moh <u>oo</u>nah
<u>kah</u>mehrah kohn <u>doo</u>-eh <u>leht</u>-tee

We'll take a room with
two beds.

**Vorremmo una camera con
un lettino.** vohr-<u>rehm</u>-moh <u>oo</u>nah
<u>kah</u>mehrah kohn oon leht-<u>tee</u>noh

We'd like a room
with one bed for a child.

Country and Culture Tip

If you take a double room, *camera doppia*, you will get a room with two beds. If you want a bed that fits two people, make sure to book a *camera matrimoniale*.

Vorrei la camera per una notte.
ohr-<u>ray</u> lah <u>kah</u>mehrah pehr <u>oo</u>nah
<u>noht</u>-teh

I'd like the room
for one night.

Vorrei la camera per due notti.
vohr-<u>ray</u> lah <u>kah</u>mehrah pehr
<u>doo</u>-eh <u>noht</u>-tee

I'd like the room
for two nights.

**Vorremmo due camere, per
piacere.** vohr-<u>rehm</u>-moh <u>doo</u>-eh
<u>kah</u>mehreh pehr pee-ah<u>cheh</u>reh

We would like two
rooms, please.

**Vorremmo le camere per una
notte.** vohr-<u>rehm</u>-moh leh
<u>kah</u>mehreh pehr <u>oo</u>nah <u>noht</u>-teh

We'd like the rooms
for one night.

**Vorremmo la camera per due
notti.** vohr-<u>rehm</u>-moh lah
<u>kah</u>mehrah pehr <u>doo</u>-eh <u>noht</u>-tee

We'd like the room
for two nights.

È pronta la camera?
eh <u>prohn</u>tah lah <u>kah</u>mehrah

Is the room ready?

Voglio stare qui per … notti.
<u>voh</u>-lyoh <u>stah</u>reh kwee pehr
… <u>noht</u>-tee

I'd like to stay for
… nights.

**Vogliamo stare qui per …
notti.** voh-<u>lyah</u>moh <u>stah</u>reh
kwee pehr … <u>noht</u>-tee

We'd like to stay for
… nights.

See page 111 for numbers.

65

Furnishings and Extras

If you have any special requests, here's how to ask for them:

Quante camere avete?
kwahnteh kahmehreh ahvehteh

How many rooms do you have? *sing. form.*

Posso avere una camera molto bella, per piacere?
pohs-soh ahvehreh oonah kahmehrah mohltoh behl-lah pehr pee-ahchehreh

Can I have a very nice room, please?

Possiamo avere una camera molto bella, per piacere?
pohs-see-ahmoh ahvehreh oonah kahmehrah mohltoh behl-lah pehr pee-ahchehreh

Can we have a very nice room, please?

Vorremmo la camera più bella che avete. vohr-rehm-moh lah kahmehrah pew behl-lah keh ahvehteh

We'd like the nicest room you have. *sing. form.*

Abbiamo bisogno di una camera grande. ahb-beeahmoh beezohnyoh dee oonah kahmehrah grahndeh

We need a large room.

Qual'è la vostra camera più bella? kwahleh lah vohstrah kahmehrah pew behl-lah

Which is the nicest room you have? *sing. form.*

Avete camere più grandi? ahvehteh kahmehreh pew grahndee

Do you have larger rooms? *sing. form.*

Avete camere più piccole? ahvehteh kahmehreh pew peak-kohleh

Do you have smaller rooms? *sing. form.*

Cosa si vede dalla camera? kohzah see vehdeh dahl-lah kahmehrah

What can we see from the room?

Vorremmo vedere … dalla camera. We'd like to see
vohr-<u>rehm</u>-moh veh<u>deh</u>reh … … from our room.
<u>dahl</u>-lah <u>kah</u>mehrah

il mare
eel <u>mahre</u>

la spiaggia
lah spee-<u>ah</u>djah

le montagne
leh mohn<u>tah</u>nyeh

Vorrei una camera con … I'd like a room with a ...
vohr-<u>ray</u> <u>oo</u>nah <u>kah</u>mehrah kohn

doccia
<u>doh</u>tchah

bagno
<u>bah</u>nyoh

toilette
twah-<u>leht</u>

TV
tee-<u>voo</u>

Posso mangiare qui? Can I eat here?
<u>pohs</u>-soh mahn<u>jah</u>reh kwee

Come vuole. As you like. *sing. form.*
<u>koh</u>meh voo-<u>oh</u>leh

Possiamo mangiare qui? Can we eat here?
pohs-see-<u>ah</u>moh mahn<u>jah</u>reh kwee

Come volete. As you like. *pl.*
<u>koh</u>meh voh<u>leh</u>teh

Quanto costa un pasto? How much is a meal?
<u>kwahn</u>toh <u>koh</u>stah oon <u>pah</u>stoh

Quanto costano i pasti? How much are the meals?
<u>kwahn</u>toh <u>koh</u>stahnoh ee <u>pah</u>stee

A che ora ci sono i pasti?
ah keh <u>oh</u>rah chee <u>soh</u>noh ee <u>pah</u>stee

What time do you serve meals?

A che ora c'è …?
ah keh <u>oh</u>rah cheh

What time is …?

la colazione
lah kohlatzee-<u>oh</u>neh

il pranzo
eel <u>prahn</u>tzoh

la cena
lah <u>cheh</u>-nah

Dove si mangia?
<u>doh</u>veh see <u>mahn</u>jah

Where do we eat?

Le faccio vedere*.
leh <u>fah</u>tchoh veh<u>deh</u>reh

I'll show you. *sing. form.*

Vi faccio vedere.
vee <u>fah</u>tchoh veh<u>deh</u>reh

I'll show you. *pl.*

If you want to check out the room before you decide, ask:

Possiamo vedere la camera?
pohs-see-<u>ah</u>moh veh<u>deh</u>reh lah <u>kah</u>mehrah

Can we see the room?

Mi può far vedere la camera?
me poo-<u>oh</u> fahr veh<u>deh</u>reh lah <u>kah</u>mehrah

Can you show me the room? *sing. form.*

---

* Idiomatic expression:
faccio vedere fahtchoh vehdehreh I show

Vorrei vedere la camera.
vohr-<u>ray</u> veh<u>deh</u>reh lah <u>kah</u>mehrah

I'd like to see the room.

Non è ancora pronta la camera?
nohn eh ahn<u>koh</u>rah <u>prohn</u>tah
lah <u>kah</u>mehrah

Is the room not ready yet?

**Questa camera è troppo grande
per me.** <u>kweh</u>stah <u>kah</u>mehrah
eh <u>trohp</u>-poh <u>grahn</u>deh pehr meh

This room is too large
for me.

Avete una camera più piccola?
ah<u>veh</u>teh <u>oo</u>nah <u>kah</u>mehrah pew
<u>peek</u>-kohlah

Do you have a smaller
room? *sing. form.*

**Questa camera è troppo piccola
per noi.** <u>kweh</u>stah <u>kah</u>mehrah eh
<u>trohp</u>-poh <u>peek</u>-kohlah pehr <u>noh</u>-ee

This room is too small
for us.

Avete una camera più grande?
ah<u>veh</u>teh <u>oo</u>nah <u>kah</u>mehrah pew
<u>grahn</u>deh

Do you have a larger
room? *sing. form.*

Avete una camera più bella?
ah<u>veh</u>teh <u>oo</u>nah <u>kah</u>mehrah pew
<u>behl</u>-lah

Do you have a nicer
room? *sing. form.*

Prices

To find out the price of the room, ask:

Quanto costa questa camera?
<u>kwahn</u>toh <u>koh</u>stah <u>kweh</u>stah <u>kah</u>mehrah

How much does this
room cost?

Quanto costa per una notte?
<u>kwahn</u>toh <u>koh</u>stah pehr <u>oo</u>nah <u>noht</u>-teh

How much is it for one
night?

Quanto costa per due notti?
<u>kwahn</u>toh <u>koh</u>stah pehr
<u>doo</u>-eh <u>noht</u>-tee

How much is it for two
nights?

È caro! eh <u>kah</u>roh — That's expensive!

È molto caro! eh <u>moh</u>ltoh <u>kah</u>roh — That's very expensive!

È troppo caro! eh <u>troh</u>p-poh <u>kah</u>roh — That's too expensive!

Quanto costa per più notti?
<u>kwahn</u>toh <u>koh</u>stah pehr
pew <u>noht</u>-tee — How much is it for more nights?

Non avete altre camere?
nohn ah<u>veh</u>teh <u>ahl</u>treh <u>kah</u>mehreh — Don't you have any other rooms? *sing. form.*

Non avete camere più piccole?
nohn ah<u>veh</u>teh <u>kah</u>mehreh
pew <u>peak</u>-kohleh — Don't you have any smaller rooms? *sing. form.*

Non c'è una camera più piccola? nohn cheh <u>oo</u>nah
<u>kah</u>mehrah pew <u>peek</u>-kohlah — Don't you have a smaller room?

Deciding

Perhaps you found what you were looking for:

Sì, questa camera mi piace molto. see <u>kweh</u>stah <u>kah</u>mehrah me pee-<u>ah</u>cheh <u>moh</u>ltoh — Yes, I like this room very much.

La camera è bellissima.
lah <u>kah</u>mehrah eh behl-<u>lees</u>-seemah — This room is beautiful.

La prendo. lah <u>prehn</u>doh — I'll take it.

Questa camera ci piace. <u>kweh</u>stah <u>kah</u>mehrah chee pee-<u>ah</u>cheh — We like this room.

La prendiamo. lah prehn-dee-<u>ah</u>moh — We'll take it.

È molto bella questa camera. eh <u>moh</u>ltoh <u>behl</u>-lah <u>kweh</u>stah <u>kah</u>mehrah — This room is very nice.

La vorremmo avere subito.
lah vohr-<u>rehm</u>-moh
ah<u>veh</u>reh <u>soo</u>beetoh

We would like to take it right away.

If you decide to continue searching for a place, you could say:

Le vostre camere costano troppo. leh <u>voh</u>streh <u>kah</u>mehreh <u>koh</u>stahnoh <u>trohp</u>-poh

Your rooms cost a lot. *sing. form.*

Le vostre camere sono troppo care. leh <u>voh</u>streh <u>kah</u>mehreh <u>soh</u>noh <u>trohp</u>-poh <u>kah</u>reh

Your rooms are too expensive. *sing. form.*

Grazie, ma voglio una camera più bella. <u>grah</u>tzee-eh mah <u>voh</u>-lyoh <u>oo</u>nah <u>kah</u>mehrah pew <u>behl</u>-lah

Thank you, but I'd like a nicer room.

Grazie, ma vogliamo una camera più bella. <u>grah</u>tzee-eh mah voh-<u>lyah</u>moh <u>oo</u>nah <u>kah</u>mehrah pew <u>behl</u>-lah

Thank you, but we'd like a nicer room.

No, non voglio questa camera, grazie. nohn <u>voh</u>-lyoh <u>kweh</u>stah <u>kah</u>mehrah <u>grah</u>tzee-eh

No, I don't want this room, thank you.

Non vogliamo questa camera, grazie. nohn voh-<u>lyah</u>moh <u>kweh</u>stah <u>kah</u>mehrah <u>grah</u>tzee-eh

We don't want this room, thank you.

Grazie che ho potuto vedere le camere. <u>grah</u>tzee-eh keh oh poh<u>too</u>toh veh<u>deh</u>reh leh <u>kah</u>mehreh

Thank you for letting me see the rooms.

Service

Someone at the front desk may tell you:

Scusi, qualcuno L'ha chiamato ♂. skoozee kwahl-**koo**noh lah key-ah**mah**toh

Excuse me, someone called for you.

Scusi, qualcuno L'ha chiamata ♀. skoozee kwahl-**koo**noh lah key-ah**mah**tah

Excuse me, someone called for you.

Scusi, c'è qualcuno che La vuole. skoozee cheh kwahl-**koo**noh keh lah voo-**oh**leh

Excuse me, there's someone asking for you.

Language Tip

If the pronouns *la* and *lo* come before a verb that starts with a vowel or a silent *h* (as in *ha*), the *a* or *o* at the end of the pronoun is often dropped:
la + ha + vista becomes *l'ha vista* (he/she has seen her)
lo + ho + fatto becomes *l'ho fatto* (I've done it)

If you want a wake-up call, say:

Ci può chiamare domani mattina? chee poo-**oh** key-ah**mah**reh doh**mah**-nee maht-**tee**nah

Can you call us tomorrow morning? *sing. form.*

A che ora? ah keh **oh**rah

At what time?

Alle ..., per piacere. **ahl**-leh ... pehr pee-ah**cheh**reh

At ... o'clock, please.

See page 111 for numbers.

If you have any special requests, say:

Vorremmo avere un letto in più*. vohr-<u>rehm</u>-moh ah<u>veh</u>reh oon <u>leht</u>-toh een pew

We'd like an additional bed.

Vorremmo avere un ... in più*. vohr-<u>rehm</u>-moh ah<u>veh</u>reh oon ... een pew

We'd like an additional ...

fon
fohn

asciugamano
ahshoo-gah<u>mah</u>noh

Abbiamo bisogno di un'altra camera. ahb-bee<u>ah</u>moh bee<u>zoh</u>nyoh dee oo-<u>nahl</u>trah <u>kah</u>mehrah

We need an additional room.

Abbiamo bisogno di un'altra ... ahb-bee<u>ah</u>moh bee<u>zoh</u>nyoh dee oo-<u>nahl</u>trah

We need an additional ...

gruccia
<u>groo</u>-tchah

saponetta
sahpoh<u>neht</u>-tah

---

* Idiomatic expression:
in più een pew

in addition

Language Tip

The article before an adjective that starts with a vowel will change in the same way as the article changes before a noun whose first letter is a vowel:

una + altra becomes *un'altra* (another; an additional ♀)
il + altro becomes *l'altro* (the other ♂)
la + altra becomes *l'altra* (the other ♀)

Posso avere un pasto, per piacere? <u>pohs</u>-soh ah<u>veh</u>reh oon <u>pah</u>stoh pehr pee-ah<u>cheh</u>reh

Could I get a meal, please?

Posso avere ..., per piacere? <u>pohs</u>-soh ah<u>veh</u>reh ... pehr pee-ah<u>cheh</u>reh

Could I get ... please?

un ferro da stiro
oon <u>fehr</u>-roh dah <u>stee</u>roh

uno shampoo
<u>oo</u>noh <u>shahm</u>-poh

If you are hungry or thirsty, ask:

Possiamo avere qualcosa da mangiare? pohs-see-<u>ah</u>moh ah<u>veh</u>reh <u>koh</u>zah dah mahn<u>jah</u>reh

Could we get something to eat?

Posso avere qualcosa da bere? <u>pohs</u>-soh ah<u>veh</u>reh kwahl-<u>koh</u>zah dah <u>beh</u>reh

Can I get something to drink?

Dove si può andare a mangiare qualcosa a quest'ora? <u>doh</u>veh see poo-<u>oh</u> ahn<u>dah</u>reh ah mahn<u>jah</u>reh kwahl-<u>koh</u>zah ah kweh<u>stoh</u>rah

Where can we get something to eat at this hour?

Dove possiamo andare a bere qualcosa a quest'ora? <u>doh</u>veh pohs-see-<u>ah</u>moh ahn<u>dah</u>reh ah <u>beh</u>reh kwahl-<u>koh</u>zah ah kweh<u>stoh</u>rah

Where can we go for a drink at this hour?

Language Tip

For easier pronunciation, the words *questo* and *questa* drop the final letter before a word beginning with a vowel: *questa* + *ora* becomes *quest'ora* (this hour/this time).

Dov'è il ... più vicino? doh<u>veh</u> eel ... pew vee<u>chee</u>noh

Where is the nearest ...?

ristorante reestoh-<u>rahn</u>teh

bar bahr

caffè kahf-<u>feh</u>

supermercato soopehr-mehr<u>kah</u>toh

Quando apre? <u>kwahn</u>doh <u>ah</u>preh

What time does it open?

È aperto oggi? eh ah-<u>peh</u>rtoh <u>oh</u>djee

Is it open today?

Complaints

If you need to complain about your neighbors:

Cosa fanno nella camera vicina? <u>koh</u>zah <u>fahn</u>-noh <u>nehl</u>-lah <u>kah</u>mehrah vee<u>chee</u>nah

What are they doing in the room next door?

C'è qualcosa che non va nella camera vicina. cheh kwahl-<u>koh</u>zah keh nohn vah <u>nehl</u>-lah <u>kah</u>mehrah vee<u>chee</u>nah

Something is not right in the room next door.

Language Tip

If an article is preceded by the prepositions *in* (in; on; at) or *di* (from; of; for; as), the two words merge:

in + *il* becomes *nel* (*nel 1999* = in 1999)
in + *la* becomes *nella* (*nella camera* = in the room)
di + *la* becomes *della* (*della camera* = of the room)
di + *il* becomes *del* (*del letto* = of the bed)

Vorremmo andare a letto ma non si può!
vohr-<u>rehm</u>-moh ahn<u>dah</u>reh ah <u>leht</u>-toh mah nohn see poo-<u>oh</u>

We would like to go to sleep now, but it's impossible!

Vorrei andare a letto!
vohr-<u>ray</u> ahn<u>dah</u>reh ah <u>leht</u>-toh

I would like to go to bed!

Fate qualcosa, per piacere!
<u>fah</u>teh kwahl-<u>koh</u>zah pehr pee-ah<u>cheh</u>reh

Do something, please!
sing. form.

Sometimes you just want to move to another room:

Voglio un'altra camera! I want a different room!
<u>voh</u>-lyoh oo-<u>nahl</u>trah <u>kah</u>mehrah

Abbiamo bisogno di un'altra We need a different room.
camera. ahb-bee<u>ah</u>moh bee<u>zoh</u>nyoh
dee oo-<u>nahl</u>trah <u>kah</u>mehrah

Domani le posso dare un'altra I can give you another
camera. doh<u>mah</u>-nee leh room tomorrow.
<u>pohs</u>-soh <u>dah</u>reh oo-<u>nahl</u>trah
<u>kah</u>mehrah

La camera non è ancora The room isn't ready yet.
pronta. lah <u>kah</u>mehrah nohn
eh ahn<u>koh</u>rah <u>prohn</u>tah

Abbiamo bisogno della camera We need the room now.
ora. ahb-bee<u>ah</u>moh bee<u>zoh</u>nyoh
<u>dehl</u>-lah <u>kah</u>mehrah <u>oh</u>rah

Ho bisogno della camera ora. I need the room now.
oh bee<u>zoh</u>nyoh <u>dehl</u>-lah
<u>kah</u>mehrah <u>oh</u>rah

Non ho molto tempo. I don't have much time.
nohn oh <u>mohl</u>toh <u>tehm</u>poh

Non abbiamo molto tempo. We don't have much
nohn ahb-bee<u>ah</u>moh <u>mohl</u>toh time.
<u>tehm</u>poh

If something in your room is broken, you can say:

Scusi, ma il letto si è Excuse me, but the
rotto. <u>skoo</u>zee mah eel bed broke.
<u>leht</u>-toh see eh <u>roht</u>-toh

Scusi, ma il ... si è rotto. <u>skoo</u>zee mah eel ... see eh <u>roht</u>-toh

Excuse me, but the ... broke.

rubinetto
roobee<u>neht</u>-toh

radiatore
rahdee-ah<u>toh</u>reh

ventilatore
vehntee-lah<u>toh</u>reh

Scusi, ma la ... si è rotta. <u>skoo</u>zee mah lah ... see eh <u>roht</u>-tah

Excuse me, but the ... broke.

TV
tee-<u>voo</u>

lampadina
lahmpah-<u>dee</u>nah

radio
<u>rah</u>dee-oh

chiave
key-<u>ah</u>veh

Possiamo avere un altro letto?
pohs-see-<u>ah</u>moh ah<u>veh</u>reh oo-<u>nahl</u>troh <u>leht</u>-toh

Could we get another bed?

Posso avere un altro letto?
<u>pohs</u>-soh ah<u>veh</u>reh oo-<u>nahl</u>troh <u>leht</u>-toh

Can I get another bed?

Può fare qualcosa subito?
poo-<u>oh</u> <u>fah</u>reh kwahl-<u>koh</u>zah <u>soo</u>beetoh

Can you do something about it now? *sing. form.*

Lo può fare per stasera?
oh poo-<u>oh</u> <u>fah</u>reh pehr stah-<u>seh</u>rah

Can you do it by tonight? *sing. form.*

Vacation Activities

Getting There

Wherever you want to go, you'll probably have to ask someone for directions eventually:

Scusi, come trovo … [place]? skoozee kohmeh trohvoh	Excuse me, how do I get to …?
Scusi, come troviamo … [place]? skoozee kohmeh trohvee-ahmoh	Excuse me, how do we get to …?
Scusi, dove si trova … [place]? skoozee dohveh see trohvah	Excuse me, where is …?
Possiamo prendere il …? pohs-see-ahmoh prehn-dehreh eel	Can we get there by …?
C'è un … qui vicino? cheh oon … kwee veecheenoh	Is there a … nearby?
A che ora c'è il … per … [place]? ah keh ohrah cheh eel … pehr	What time does the … go to …?

bus
boos

metrò
mehtroh

treno
trehnoh

tram
trahm

A che ora c'è? ah keh ohrah cheh	What time does it leave?
Che ore sono? keh ohreh sohnoh	What time is it?
Scusi, mi può dire che ore sono? skoozee mee poo-oh deereh keh ohreh sohnoh	Excuse me, can you tell me what time it is? *sing. form.*

Quanto tempo ci vuole*? How long does it take?
kwahntoh tehmpoh chee voo-ohleh

Shopping

If you need to find a particular shop, ask for it with this phrase:

Scusi, dov'è … più vicino? Excuse me, where is the
skoozee dohveh … pew nearest …?
veecheenoh

il macellaio
eel mahchel-lahee-oh

il mercato
eel mehrkahtoh

l'ottico
loht-teekoh

il panificio
eel pahnee-feechoh

il fruttivendolo
eel froot-teevehn-
dohloh

il gioieliere
eel joy-ehl-lee-
ehreh

Scusi, dove trovo regali qui Excuse me, where can I
vicino? skoozee dohveh trohvoh buy presents around here?
rehgahlee kwee veecheenoh

---

* Idiomatic expression:
ci vuole chee voo-ohleh   it takes; one needs

Scusi, dove trovo ... qui vicino? <u>skoo</u>zee doh<u>veh</u> <u>troh</u>voh ... kwee vee<u>chee</u>noh

Excuse me, where can I buy ... around here?

abbigliamento
ahb-beelyah-<u>mehn</u>toh

pellicole
pehl-<u>lee</u>kohleh

fiori
fee-<u>oh</u>ree

scarpe
<u>skahr</u>peh

sigarette
seegah<u>reht</u>-teh

giornali
johr<u>nah</u>lee

You'll need to know the opening times:

A che ora aprite?
ah keh <u>oh</u>rah ah<u>pree</u>teh

What time do you open?
sing. form.

Avete aperto il ...?
ah<u>veh</u>teh ah<u>pehr</u>toh eel

Are you open on ...?
sing. form.

See page 112 for days of the week.

In quali giorni non avete aperto?
een <u>kwah</u>lee <u>johr</u>nee nohn ah<u>veh</u>teh ah-<u>pehr</u>toh

What days of the week are you not open?
sing. form.

Country and Culture Tip

Most Italian shops are open between 8:30 and 9:00 am, and stay open until lunch at around 1:00 pm. They re-open in the afternoon around 3:00 or 4:00 pm, and stay open until 8:00 pm. Supermarkets in the cities are often closed on Thursday afternoons, while clothing shops and hairdressers are closed on Mondays. In tourist centers, many shops will have extended hours during the summer months.

Let's go shopping:

Che taglia è? keh <u>tahl</u>yah eh — What size is this?

È la … [size]. eh lah — That's size …

Che taglia ha? keh <u>tahl</u>yah ah — What size do you wear? *sing. form.*

Ho la … [size]. oh lah — I wear size …

In Stati Uniti* ho la … een <u>stah</u>tee oo<u>nee</u>tee oh lah — In the States I wear a …

See page 111 for numbers.

Country and Culture Tip

Remember that Italian sizes differ from sizes in the US and the UK. For women, an Italian size 42 would be a US size 8/10, or a UK size 30/32. The same applies for men; an Italian size 58 suit corresponds with a US size 40.

---

* **Gran-Bretagna** grahn breh<u>tahn</u>yah — Great Britain
Canada kah-nah-<u>dah</u> — Canada

Vorrei qualcosa di bello per la sera. vohr-<u>ray</u> kwahl-<u>koh</u>zah dee <u>behl</u>-loh pehr lah <u>seh</u>rah

I want something nice for the evening.

Questo potrebbe andare bene. <u>kweh</u>stoh poh<u>trehb</u>-beh ahn<u>dah</u>reh <u>beh</u>neh

That could fit me.

Lo vediamo subito. loh vehdee-<u>ah</u>moh <u>soo</u>beetoh

We'll see.

Le va bene questo? leh vah <u>beh</u>neh <u>kweh</u>stoh

Does it fit you? *sing. form.*

Le va bene questa taglia? leh vah <u>beh</u>neh <u>kweh</u>stah <u>tah</u>lyah

Does this size fit you? *sing. form.*

No, è troppo piccolo. noh eh <u>trohp</u>-poh <u>peak</u>-kohloh

No, it's too small.

No, è troppo grande. noh eh <u>trohp</u>-poh <u>grah</u>ndeh

No, it's too large.

Questo è troppo piccolo. <u>kweh</u>stoh eh <u>trohp</u>-poh <u>peak</u>-kohloh

That's too small.

Questo è troppo grande. <u>kweh</u>stoh eh <u>trohp</u>-poh <u>grah</u>ndeh

That's too large.

Ho bisogno di una taglia in più.[*] oh bee<u>zohn</u>yoh dee <u>oo</u>nah <u>tah</u>lyah een pew

I need it one size larger.

C'è più piccolo? cheh pew <u>peak</u>-kohloh

Is this also available in a smaller size?

---

[*] Idiomatic expression: **in più** een pew

more, in addition

Mi sta bene? mee stah <u>beh</u>neh

Does it look good on me?

Mi sta bene questo?
mee stah <u>beh</u>neh <u>kweh</u>stoh

Does this look good
on me?

Sì, le sta bene.
see leh stah <u>beh</u>neh

Yes, it looks good on you.
sing. form.

Sì, le sta molto bene.
see leh stah <u>mohl</u>toh <u>beh</u>neh

Yes, it looks very good
on you. *sing. form.*

Mi sta meglio questo?
mee stah <u>meh</u>lyoh <u>kweh</u>stoh

Does this look better?

Sì, le sta ancora meglio.
see leh stah ahn<u>koh</u>rah <u>meh</u>lyoh

Yes, this looks even
better on you. *sing. form.*

No, non le sta meglio.
noh nohn leh stah <u>meh</u>lyoh

No, this doesn't look
better on you. *sing. form.*

Questo è bellissimo!
<u>kweh</u>stoh eh behl-<u>lees</u>-seemoh

This is beautiful!

Lo prendo! loh <u>prehn</u>doh

I'll take it!

If you want to buy a traditional Italian souvenir to take home for
your friends and relatives:

Posso vedere? <u>pohs</u>-soh
veh<u>deh</u>reh

May I see this?

Cos'è questo?
koh<u>zeh</u> <u>kweh</u>stoh

What is this?

Ho bisogno di un regalo bello.
oh bee<u>zohn</u>yoh dee oon reh<u>gah</u>loh
<u>behl</u>-loh

I need a nice present.

Vorrei un regalo bello ma non troppo caro. vohr-ray oon reh<u>gah</u>loh <u>behl</u>-loh mah nohn <u>trohp</u>-poh <u>kah</u>roh

I'd like a nice present that isn't too expensive.

Country and Culture Tip

If you're looking for presents to bring back home, try a good bottle of wine (a *Chianti* or *Barolo* for example), or olive oil (*extra vergine* of course), or an unusual type of pasta. If you want to spend a little more on your present consider Italian leather products or pottery.

Entertainment

Ora cosa facciamo?
<u>oh</u>rah <u>koh</u>zah fah-<u>tchah</u>moh

What do we do now?

Ora cosa si potrebbe fare?
<u>oh</u>rah <u>koh</u>zah see poh<u>trehb</u>-beh <u>fah</u>reh

What can we do now?

Cosa facciamo stasera?
<u>koh</u>zah fah-<u>tchah</u>moh stah-<u>seh</u>rah

What are we going to do tonight?

Dove andiamo?
<u>doh</u>veh ahndee-<u>ah</u>moh

Where do we go?

Andiamo … ahndee-<u>ah</u>moh

Let's go to the …

Vorrei andare …
vohr-<u>ray</u> ahn<u>dah</u>reh

I'd like to go to the ...

al museo
ahl moo<u>zeh</u>-oh

a teatro
ah teh-<u>ah</u>troh

all'opera
ahl-<u>loh</u>pehrah

al concerto
ahl kohn<u>chehr</u>toh

Dove posso prendere i biglietti?
<u>doh</u>veh <u>pohs</u>-soh <u>prehn</u>-dehreh ee bee-<u>lyeht</u>-tee

Where can I buy tickets?

Ho bisogno di biglietti molto buoni. oh bee<u>zohn</u>yoh dee bee-<u>lyeht</u>-tee <u>mohl</u>toh <u>bwoh</u>nee

I need very good seats.

Vorrei biglietti non troppo cari.
vohr-<u>ray</u> bee-<u>lyeht</u>-tee nohn <u>trohp</u>-poh <u>kah</u>ree

I'd like tickets that are not too expensive.

Quanto costano i biglietti?
<u>kwahn</u>toh <u>koh</u>stahnoh ee bee-<u>lyeht</u>-tee

How much are the tickets?

A che ora è? ah keh <u>oh</u>rah eh

What time does it start?

A che ora andiamo?
ah keh <u>oh</u>rah ahndee-<u>ah</u>mo

What time do we go?

Going Out to Eat

Before you go out to eat, you have to set a time:

A che ora vorresti mangiare?
ah keh <u>oh</u>rah vohr-<u>reh</u>stee
mahn<u>jah</u>reh

What time would you
like to eat? *sing. inform.*

**Quando vuole mangiare
qualcosa?** <u>kwah</u>ndoh voo-<u>oh</u>leh
mahn<u>jah</u>reh kwahl-<u>koh</u>zah

What time would
you like to eat?
sing. form.

A che ora mangi la sera?
ah keh <u>oh</u>rah <u>mahn</u>jee lah <u>seh</u>rah

What time do you
eat dinner? *sing. inform.*

Andiamo a mangiare ora?
ahndee-<u>ah</u>moh ah mahn<u>jah</u>reh
<u>oh</u>rah

Should we go to eat now?

**Possiamo avere qualcosa da
mangiare?** pohs-see-<u>ah</u>moh
ah<u>veh</u>reh kwahl-<u>koh</u>zah dah
mahn<u>jah</u>reh

Can we have something
to eat?

You'll also want to think about what, and how much, to eat:

Cosa vorresti mangiare?
<u>koh</u>zah vohr-<u>reh</u>stee mahn<u>jah</u>reh

What would you like to
eat? *sing. inform.*

Cosa vuole da mangiare?
<u>koh</u>zah voo-<u>oh</u>leh dah mahn<u>jah</u>reh

What would you like
to eat? *sing. form.*

Cosa prende? <u>koh</u>zah <u>preh</u>ndeh

What will you have?
sing. form.

Vorrei … vohr-<u>ray</u>   I'd like …

una minestra   **del salame**   **un'insalata**   **delle olive**
<u>oo</u>nah   dehl sah<u>lah</u>-meh   ooneen-sah<u>lah</u>tah   <u>dehl</u>-leh
mee<u>neh</u>strah   oh<u>lee</u>veh

Vorrei … con … vohr-<u>ray</u> … kohn   I'd like … with …

una cotoletta   **il pesce**   **la carne di vitello**
<u>oo</u>nah kohtoh<u>leh</u>t-tah   eel <u>peh</u>sheh   lah <u>kahr</u>neh dee
                                      vee<u>teh</u>l-loh

le patatine   **le carote**   **le patate**   **il riso**
leh pahtah-<u>tee</u>neh   leh kah<u>roh</u>teh   leh pah<u>tah</u>teh   eel <u>ree</u>zoh

---

Country and Culture Tip

In Italy, a full meal consists of an appetizer, followed by
il primo (a noodle or rice dish), the main course *il secondo*
(something with fish or meat) and a dessert.

E cosa vuole da bere?
eh <u>koh</u>zah voo-<u>ohl</u>eh dah <u>beh</u>reh

And what would you like to drink? *sing. form.*

Vuole bere qualcosa?
voo-<u>ohl</u>eh <u>beh</u>reh kwahl-<u>koh</u>zah

Would you like something to drink? *sing. form.*

Vorrei … vohr-<u>ray</u>

I'd like …

un'acqua
on<u>ahk</u>-kwah

un bicchiere di vino rosso
oon beek-key<u>eh</u>reh dee <u>vee</u>noh <u>roh</u>s-soh

un bicchiere di vino bianco
oon beek-key<u>eh</u>reh dee <u>vee</u>noh bee-<u>ah</u>nkoh

una birra
<u>oo</u>nah <u>beer</u>-rah

Non mangio tanto.
nohn <u>mahn</u>joh <u>tahn</u>toh

I don't eat much.

Non posso mangiare tanto stasera. nohn <u>pohs</u>-soh mahn<u>jah</u>reh <u>tahn</u>toh stah-<u>seh</u>rah

I can't eat much tonight.

Posso avere ancora qualcosa di questo? <u>pohs</u>-soh ah<u>veh</u>reh ahn<u>koh</u>rah kwahl-<u>koh</u>zah dee <u>kweh</u>stoh

Could I have some more of this?

Vuole ancora qualcosa?
voo-<u>ohl</u>eh ahn<u>koh</u>rah kwahl-<u>koh</u>zah

Do you want anything else? *sing. form.*

No, grazie. Non posso più mangiare niente. noh grahtzee-eh nohn pohs-soh pew mahnjahreh nee-ehnteh

No thanks. I can't eat any more.

Unfortunately, there are times where you need to complain:

Non è quello che voglio.
nohn eh kwehl-loh keh voh-lyoh

This is not what I want.

Scusi, ma questo non è buono. skoozee mah kwehstoh nohn eh bwohnoh

Excuse me, but this is not good.

Scusi, ma non è buono per niente*. skoozee mah nohn eh bwohnoh pehr nee-ehnteh

Excuse me, but this is not good at all.

Non lo mangio.
nohn loh mahnjoh

I'm not going to eat this.

Non lo pago. nohn loh pahgoh

I won't pay for this.

In the Bar

Vuole ancora qualcosa da bere? voo-ohleh ahnkohrah kwahl-kohzah dah behreh

Do you want anything else to drink? *sing. form.*

Sì, ma vorrei pagare per me. see mah vohr-ray pahgahreh pehr meh

Yes, but I want to pay for it myself.

Vorrei pagare. vohr-ray pahgahreh

I'd like to pay.

---

* Idiomatic expression:
   non ... per niente nohn pehr nee-ehnteh not at all

Alla tua! ahl-lah <u>too</u>ah

To your health! *sing. inform.*

Alla vostra! ahl-lah <u>voh</u>strah

To your health! *pl.*

No grazie, non bevo più niente.
noh <u>grah</u>tzee-eh nohn <u>beh</u>voh
pew nee-<u>ehn</u>teh

No thanks, I'm not going to drink anymore.

Ho bevuto troppo.
oh beh<u>voo</u>toh <u>trohp</u>-poh

I had too much to drink.

Country and Culture Tip

An Italian *bar* is not the same as an American or British bar. A typical *bar* usually has a counter and a few small tables where Italians drink their morning *cappuccino* and eat their breakfast *brioche* (roll or pastry). At night, it's common to go to a *bar* for a glass of wine or an *espresso*.

Flirting

If you want to start a conversation with someone:

Sei qui con qualcuno?
say kwee kohn kwahl-<u>koo</u>noh

Are you here with someone? *sing. inform.*

È qui con qualcuno?
eh kwee kohn kwahl-<u>koo</u>noh

Are you here with someone? *sing. form.*

Ti ho visto ieri sera.
tee oh <u>vee</u>stoh ee-<u>eh</u>ree <u>seh</u>rah

I saw you last night. *sing. inform.*

Andiamo a mangiare stasera?
ahndee-<u>ah</u>moh ah mahn<u>jah</u>reh
stah-<u>seh</u>rah

Shall we go out for dinner tonight?

Hai tempo stasera?
ahee <u>teh</u>mpoh stah-<u>seh</u>rah

Do you have time this evening? *sing. inform.*

Ha tempo domani sera?
ah <u>teh</u>mpoh doh<u>mah</u>-nee <u>seh</u>rah

Do you have time tomorrow evening? *sing. form.*

Sì, ho tempo. see oh <u>teh</u>mpoh

Yes, I have time.

Grazie tanto. <u>grah</u>tzee-eh <u>tahn</u>toh

Thank you very much.

Ci vediamo ancora?
chee vehdee-<u>ah</u>moh ahn<u>koh</u>rah

Will we see each other again?

Ci vediamo domani?
chee vehdee-<u>ah</u>moh doh<u>mah</u>-nee

Will we see each other tomorrow?

Country and Culture Tip

To impress a woman, Italian men like to pay for things on the first few dates. When you go out with friends, however, it's the custom to split the bill evenly.

If you like someone and want to move beyond friendly conversation, you can say:

È bello stare con te.
eh <u>beh</u>l-loh <u>stah</u>reh kohn teh

It is nice to be with you. *sing. inform.*

Sei bellissima ♀.
say behl-<u>lees</u>-seemah

You are very good-looking. *sing. inform.*

Sei bellissimo ♂.
say behl-<u>lees</u>-seemoh

You are very handsome. *sing. inform.*

Mi piaci molto.
mee pee-<u>ah</u>chee <u>mohl</u>toh

I like you very much. *sing. inform.*

Mi piace stare con te.
mee pee-<u>ah</u>cheh <u>stah</u>reh kohn teh

I like being with you.
sing. inform.

If you want to break it off, you can do it gently or firmly:

Grazie, ma ho troppe cose da fare. <u>grah</u>tzee-eh mah oh <u>trohp</u>-peh <u>koh</u>zeh dah <u>fah</u>reh

Thank you, but I am very busy.

No grazie, ho altro da fare! noh <u>grah</u>tzee-eh oh <u>ah</u>ltroh dah <u>fah</u>reh

No thanks, I have something else to do!

Scusa, ma sto con qualcuno. <u>skoo</u>zah mah stoh kohn kwahl-<u>koo</u>noh

I am sorry, but I am with someone else.

Non vuoi capire?
nohn voo-<u>oh</u>ee kah<u>pee</u>reh

Don't you understand?
sing. inform.

Ho detto di no.
oh <u>deht</u>-toh dee noh

I said no.

Problems and Emergencies

Asking for Help

Mi potrebbe aiutare?
mee poh<u>trehb</u>-beh ahyou-<u>tah</u>reh

Could you help me?
sing. form.

Ci potrebbe aiutare?
chee poh<u>trehb</u>-beh ahyou-<u>tah</u>reh

Could you help us?
sing. form.

Mi può aiutare, per piacere?
mee poo-<u>oh</u> ahyou-<u>tah</u>reh pehr
pee-ah<u>cheh</u>reh

Can you help me, please?
sing. form.

Ho bisogno di aiuto!
oh bee<u>zoh</u>nyoh dee ah<u>you</u>toh

I need help!

Aiuto! ah<u>you</u>toh

Help!

**Chiamate qualcuno che ci può
aiutare!** key-ah<u>mah</u>teh kwahl-
<u>koo</u>noh keh chee poo-<u>oh</u> ahyou-<u>tah</u>reh

Get someone who can
help us! *pl.*

**Chiama qualcuno che ci può
aiutare!** key-ah<u>mah</u> kwahl-<u>koo</u>noh
keh chee poo-<u>oh</u> ahyou-<u>tah</u>reh

Get someone who can
help us! *sing. inform.*

E vai! eh <u>vah</u>-ee

Go on, get lost!
sing. inform.

Fate qualcosa! <u>fah</u>teh kwahl-<u>koh</u>zah

Do something! *pl.*

Ci deve aiutare subito.
chee <u>deh</u>veh ahyou-<u>tah</u>reh
<u>soo</u>beetoh

You've got to help us
now. *sing. form.*

Accidents

Hopefully, you won't need to use any of these phrases:

Tutto bene? <u>toot</u>-toh <u>beh</u>neh — Everything OK?

Stai bene? <u>stah</u>-ee <u>beh</u>neh — Are you OK? *sing. inform.*

Sta bene? stah <u>beh</u>neh — Are you OK? *sing. form.*

Non ti sei rotto niente ♂?
nohn tee say <u>roht</u>-toh nee-<u>ehn</u>teh — Are you sure you didn't break anything? *sing. inform.*

Non ti sei rotta niente ♀?
nohn tee say <u>roht</u>-tah nee-<u>ehn</u>teh — Are you sure you didn't break anything? *sing. form.*

Non ti fa male niente?
nohn tee fah <u>mah</u>leh nee-<u>ehn</u>teh — Are you sure you're not hurt? *sing. inform.*

Non le fa male niente?
nohn leh fah <u>mah</u>leh nee-<u>ehn</u>teh — Are you sure you're not hurt? *sing. form.*

If you are in an accident, one of the first questions is usually about whose fault it was:

Non ho fatto niente!
nohn oh <u>faht</u>-toh nee-<u>ehn</u>teh

I did nothing!

Siete stati voi ♂!
see-<u>eh</u>teh <u>stah</u>tee <u>voh</u>-ee

You did it! *pl.*

Siete state voi ♀!
see-<u>eh</u>teh <u>stah</u>teh <u>voh</u>-ee

You did it! *pl.*

Non siamo stati noi ♂!
nohn see-<u>ah</u>moh <u>stah</u>tee <u>noh</u>-ee

It wasn't us!

Non siamo state noi ♀!
nohn see-<u>ah</u>moh <u>stah</u>teh <u>noh</u>-ee

It wasn't us!

Ho visto tutto. oh <u>vee</u>stoh <u>toot</u>-toh I saw everything.

Non mi ha visto?
nohn mee ah <u>vee</u>stoh

Didn't you see me?
sing. form.

Chiami ..., per piacere.
key-<u>ah</u>mee ... pehr pee-ah<u>cheh</u>reh

Please call ...

il soccorso stradale
eel sohk-<u>kohr</u>soh strah<u>dah</u>leh

l'ambulanza
lahmboo<u>lahnt</u>zah

la polizia
lah pohlee<u>tzee</u>-ah

Loss and Theft

Ho perso il biglietto.   I lost my ticket.
oh <u>pehr</u>soh eel bee-<u>lyeht</u>-toh

Ho perso il ...   I lost my ...
oh <u>pehr</u>soh eel

l'anello   **il portafoglio**   **il passaporto**   **l'orologio**
lah<u>nehl</u>-loh   eel pohrtah-<u>foh</u>-lyoh   eel pahs-sah<u>pohr</u>toh   lohroh-<u>lohj</u>oh

Qualcuno ha rotto ...   Somebody damaged ...
kwahl-<u>koo</u>noh ah <u>roht</u>-toh

la macchina   **la roulotte**
lah <u>mahk</u>-keynah   lah roo<u>loht</u>

il camper   **la tenda**
eel <u>kahm</u>pehr   lah <u>tehn</u>dah

Hanno preso tutte le cose!
ahn-noh prehzoh toot-teh leh kohzeh

They took everything!

Non c'è più niente.
nohn cheh pew nee-ehnteh

There's nothing left.

Visiting the Doctor

Cosa posso fare per voi?
kohzah pohs-soh fahreh pehr voh-ee

What can I do for you? *pl.*

Non sto bene per niente.
nohn stoh behneh pehr nee-ehnteh

I don't feel well at all.

Ho male qui … [pointing].
oh mahleh kwee

It hurts here.

C'è qualcosa che non va con …
cheh kwahl-kohzah keh nohn
vah kohn

There's something wrong with my …

il cuore
eel kwohreh

il braccio
eel brah-tchoh

la gamba
lah gahmbah

Cosa posso fare?
kohzah pohs-soh fahreh

What can I do?

Country and Culture Tip

Make sure you contact your health insurance company before you leave to find out if you're covered for hospital stays or doctor's visits. If you've booked an all-inclusive trip, consider taking out insurance for your stay abroad so that all medical costs will be covered.

Difficulties

If someone is bothering you, here's how to talk back:

Non ho tempo. nohn oh <u>teh</u>mpoh — I don't have time.

Non La voglio vicino!
nohn lah <u>voh</u>-lyoh veeche<u>e</u>noh — I don't want you near me! *sing. form.*

Non capisce? nohn kah<u>pee</u>sheh — Don't you get it? *sing. form.*

Non mi dare nomi!
nohn mee <u>dah</u>reh <u>noh</u>mee — Don't insult me! *sing. inform.*

Ma cosa vuoi? mah <u>koh</u>zah voo-<u>ohee</u> — What do you want anyhow? *sing. inform.*

Ma cosa vuole?
mah <u>koh</u>zah voo-<u>oh</u>leh — What do you want anyhow? *sing. form.*

If you're lost, don't be afraid to ask for help:

Scusi, mi sono perso ♂.
<u>skoo</u>zee mee <u>soh</u>noh <u>pehr</u>soh — Excuse me, I'm lost.

Scusi, mi sono persa ♀.
<u>skoo</u>zee mee <u>soh</u>noh <u>pehr</u>sah — Excuse me, I'm lost.

Non sei di qui? nohn say dee kwee — You're not from here? *sing. inform.*

È di qui? eh dee kwee — Are you from here? *sing. form.*

Ci siamo persi. chee see-<u>ah</u>moh <u>pehr</u>see — We're lost.

Ci può aiutare? chee poo-<u>oh</u> ahyou-<u>tah</u>reh — Can you help us? *sing. form.*

Voglio andare a ... [place]. <u>voh</u>-lyoh ahn<u>dah</u>reh ah — I want to go to ...

Vogliamo andare a ... [place]. voh-l<u>yah</u>moh ahn<u>dah</u>reh ah — We want to go to ...

Dove sono? <u>doh</u>veh <u>soh</u>noh — Where am I?

Problems

If you happen to break or damage anything, apologize by saying:

Ho rotto il letto. oh <u>roht</u>-toh eel <u>leht</u>-toh — I broke the bed.

Ho rotto ... oh <u>roht</u>-toh — I broke the ...

la TV lah tee-<u>voo</u>

il bicchiere eel beek-key<u>eh</u>reh

gli occhiali lyee ohk-key-<u>ah</u>lee

la videocamera lah <u>vee</u>dehoh-<u>kah</u>mehrah

Scusa. <u>skoo</u>zah

I'm sorry. *sing. inform.*

Mi scusi tanto.
mee <u>skoo</u>zee <u>tahn</u>toh

I'm so sorry. *sing. form.*

Ci scusi tanto.
chee <u>skoo</u>zee <u>tahn</u>toh

We're so sorry. *sing. form.*

Lo posso pagare?
oh <u>pohs</u>-soh pah<u>gah</u>reh

Can I pay for it?

A

a ah to; at; in
abbiamo ahb-bee<u>ah</u>moh we have
abbiamo bisogno di ahb-bee<u>ah</u>moh bee<u>zoh</u>nyoh dee we need/require
l'abbigliamento *m* lahb-beelyah-<u>meh</u>ntoh clothing
l'acqua *f* l<u>ah</u>k-kwah water
aiuta ahy<u>oo</u>tah he/she/it helps; you help *sing. form.*
aiutare ahyou-<u>tah</u>reh to help
aiutarsi ahyou-<u>tah</u>rsee to help oneself
aiutarti ahyou-<u>tah</u>rtee help you
aiutate ahyou-<u>tah</u>teh you help *pl.*
aiutato ahyou-<u>tah</u>toh helped
aiuti ahy<u>oo</u>tee you help *sing. inform.*
aiuto ahy<u>oo</u>toh I help
l'aiuto *m* lahy<u>oo</u>toh help
al ahl to; at; in
l'albergo *m* lahl<u>beh</u>rgoh accommodation; hotel
all' ahl' to; at; in
alle <u>ah</u>l-leh at *(time)*
altro <u>ah</u>ltroh another; additional
l'ambulanza *f* lahmboo-<u>lahn</u>tzah ambulance
ancora ahn<u>koh</u>rah still; yet
andare ahn<u>dah</u>reh to go
andate ahn<u>dah</u>teh you go *pl.*
andato ahn<u>dah</u>toh gone
andiamo ahndee-<u>ah</u>moh we go
l'anello *m* lah<u>neh</u>l-loh ring
l'aperitivo *m* lah-pehree-<u>tee</u>voh aperitif

aperto ah-<u>peh</u>rtoh open
apre <u>ah</u>preh he/she/it opens
aprire ah<u>pree</u>reh to open
aprirsi ah<u>pree</u>r-see to open up
aprite ah<u>pree</u>teh you *pl.* open
arrivederci ahr-reeveh-<u>dehr</u>chee good-bye
arrivederLa ahr-reeveh-<u>dehr</u>lah good-bye
l'asciugamano *m* lahshoo-gah<u>mah</u>noh towel
avere ah<u>veh</u>reh to have
avete ah<u>veh</u>teh you have *pl.*

B

il bagno eel <u>bah</u>nyoh bathroom; bath
il bar eel bahr bar
bel(lo) behl; <u>behl</u>-loh nice
bellissimo behl-<u>lees</u>-seemoh beautiful
bene <u>beh</u>neh well
bere <u>beh</u>reh to drink
bevo <u>beh</u>voh I drink
bevuto beh<u>voo</u>toh drunk
bianco bee-<u>ahn</u>koh white
il bicchiere eel beek-key<u>eh</u>reh glass
il biglietto eel bee-<u>lyeh</u>t-toh ticket *(train)*
la birra lah <u>beer</u>-rah beer
bisogno: avere bisogno di ah<u>veh</u>reh bee<u>zoh</u>nyoh dee to need
il braccio eel <u>brah</u>-tchoh arm
la brioche lah bree-<u>ohsh</u> croissant
brutto <u>broot</u>-toh ugly; terrible

buon(o) bwohn;
bwohnoh good
buongiorno bwohn-
johrnoh good morning
il bus eel boos bus

C

il caffèè eel kahf-feh coffee;
café
la camera lah kahmehrah
room
la camera doppia lah kahmehrah dohp-pee-ah room
with two beds
la camera matrimoniale lah
kahmehrah mahtree-mohnee-
ahleh double room
la camicia lah
kahmeechah shirt
il campeggio eel kahmpehdjoh camping site
il camper eel kahmpehr R.V.
il cane eel kahneh dog
capire kahpeereh to understand
capirlo kahpeerloh understand him/it
capirsi kahpeersee to understand one another
capisce kahpeesheh he/
she/it understands; you understand *sing. form.*
capisci kahpeeshee you understand *sing. inform.*
capisco kahpeeskoh I understand
capito kahpeetoh understood
il cappello eel kahp-pehl-
loh hat

il cappuccino eel kahp-poo-
cheeno cappuccino
la carne lah kahrneh meat
la carne di vitello lah kahrneh
dee veetehl-loh veal
caro kahroh expensive
la carota lah kahrohtah carrot
la carta geografica lah
kahrtah jehoh-
grahfeekah map
la carta stradale lah kahrtah
strahdahleh road map
il casco eel kahskoh helmet
il casinò eel
kahzeenoh casino
c'è cheh there is
la cena lah cheh-nah dinner
che keh which; who; that
chiama key-ahmah he/she/it
calls; you call *sing. form.*
si chiama see key-
ahmah he/she/it is called;
you are called *sing. form.*
chiamare key-ahmahreh to
call *(on the phone)*
chiamarsi key-ahmahrsee to
be called
chiamate key-ahmahteh you
call *(on the phone) pl.*
vi chiamate vee key-
ahmahteh you are called *pl.*
chiamato key-ahmahtoh called
chiami key-ahmee you call
sing. inform. call!
ti chiami tee key-ah-mee you
are called *sing. inform.*
chiamo: mi chiamo mee key-
ahmoh I am called
la chiave lah key-ahveh key
la chiesa lah key-ehzah church

ci <u>chee</u> us; there
ciao <u>chah</u>-oh hello; bye
il cioccolato eel chohk-
kohl<u>ah</u>toh chocolate
cioccolata calda
chohk-koh<u>lah</u>tah <u>kah</u>ldah
hot chocolate
ci si vede chee see
<u>veh</u>deh we'll see each other
ci sono chee <u>soh</u>noh there are
ci vuole chee voo-<u>oh</u>leh one
needs
la colazione lah kohlahtzee-
<u>oh</u>neh breakfast
come <u>koh</u>meh how
con kohn with
il concerto eel
kohn<u>cheh</u>rtoh concert
cosa <u>koh</u>zah what
la cosa lah <u>koh</u>zah thing; item
costa <u>koh</u>stah it costs
costano <u>koh</u>stahnoh they
cost
costare koh<u>stah</u>reh to cost
il costume eel
koh<u>stoo</u>meh swimsuit
la cotoletta lah kohtoh<u>leh</u>t-
tah chop
la cravatta lah krah<u>vah</u>t-tah tie
il cuore eel <u>kwoh</u>reh heart

D

da dah from; since
dal dahl from the; since
dall' dahl from; since; at (*before vowels*)
dalla <u>dahl</u>-lah from the; since
the; at the

dalle <u>dahl</u>-leh from the *pl.*;
since the *pl.*; at the *pl.*
dare <u>dah</u>reh to give
del dehl of/from the
delle <u>dehl</u>-leh of/from the *pl.*
detto <u>deht</u>-toh said
di dee from; of
dice <u>dee</u>-cheh he/she/it says;
you say *sing. form.*
dico <u>dee</u>koh I say
di mattina dee maht-<u>tee</u>nah in
the morning
dire <u>dee</u>reh to say
la discoteca lah deeskoh-
<u>teh</u>kah disco; nightclub
di sera dee <u>seh</u>rah in the
evening
la doccia lah <u>doh</u>tchah shower
domani doh<u>mah</u>-nee tomorrow
dove <u>doh</u>veh where
due <u>doo</u>-eh two

E

e eh and
è eh he/she/it is; you are *sing.
form.*
esserci <u>ehs</u>-sehrchee to be
there
essere <u>ehs</u>-sehreh to be

F

fa fah he/she/it does/makes;
you do/make *sing. form.*
facciamo fah-<u>tchah</u>moh we
do/make
faccio <u>fah</u>-tchoh I do/make

faccio: mi faccio capire mee fah-tchoh kah<u>pee</u>reh I make myself understood

faccio vedere <u>fah</u>-tchoh veh<u>deh</u>reh I show

fanno <u>fahn</u>-noh they do/make

fare <u>fah</u>reh to do; make

far male fahr <u>mah</u>leh to hurt; to be in pain

farsi capire <u>fahr</u>see kah<u>pee</u>reh to make oneself understood

far vedere fahr veh<u>deh</u>reh to show

fate <u>fah</u>teh you do/make *pl.*

fatto <u>faht</u>-toh done/made

il ferro da stiro eel <u>fehr</u>-roh dah <u>stee</u>roh hot iron

il film eel feelm movie

il fiore eel fee-<u>oh</u>reh flower

il fon eel fohn hair dryer

il formaggio eel fohr<u>mah</u>djoh cheese

il fruttivendolo eel froot-tee<u>vehn</u>-dohloh fruit seller

G

la gamba lah <u>gahm</u>bah leg

il gatto eel <u>gaht</u>-toh cat

la giacca lah <u>jahk</u>-kah jacket

il gioielliere eel joy-ehl-lee-<u>eh</u>reh jeweler

il giornale eel johr<u>nah</u>leh newspaper

il giorno eel <u>johr</u>noh day

gli *m* lyee the

la gonna lah <u>gohn</u>-nah skirt

Gran Bretagna grahn breh<u>tah</u>nyah Great Britain

grande <u>grahn</u>deh big; large

grazie <u>grah</u>tzee-eh thank you

la gruccia lah <u>groo</u>-tchah coat hanger

H

ha ah he/she/it has; you have *sing. form.*

hai <u>a</u>hee you have *sing. inform.*

hanno <u>ahn</u>-noh they have

ho oh I have

ho bisogno di oh bee<u>zoh</u>nyoh dee I need

l'hotel *m* loh<u>tehl</u> hotel

I

i *m* ee the

ieri ee-<u>eh</u>ree yesterday

il eel *m* the

in een in; on; at

in più een pew in addition

l'insalata *f* leensah-<u>lah</u>tah salad

L

l' l the (*before vowels*)

la lah the; she

La lah you *sing. form.*

la lampadina lah lahmpah-<u>dee</u>nah light bulb

le *f* leh the *pl.;* you *pl.;* them

il lettino eel leht-<u>tee</u>noh children's bed

il letto eel <u>leht</u>-toh bed

la limonata lah leemoh-<u>nah</u>tah lemonade

lo loh the; him; it

M

ma mah but
la macchina lah mahk-keynah car
il macellaio eel mahchel-lahyoh butcher
male mahleh bad
mangi mahnjee you eat *sing. inform.*
mangia mahnjah he/she/it eats; you eat *sing. form.*
mangiare mahnjahreh to eat
mangiato mahnjahtoh eaten
mangio mahnjoh I eat
la mano lah mahnoh hand
il mare eel mahreh sea
la marmellata lah mahrmehl-lahtah jam
la mattina lah maht-teenah morning
me meh me/to me
meglio mehlyoh better
meno mehnoh less; minus
il mercato eel mehrkahtoh market
il metrò eel mehtroh subway
mezza mehtzah half
mi mee me/to me
la minestra lah meenehstrah soup
molto mohltoh much
la montagna lah mohntahnyah mountain; mountain range
la moto lah mohtoh motorcycle
il museo eel moozeh-oh museum

N

nel *m* nehl in the
nella *f* nehl-lah in the
niente nee-ehnteh nothing
no noh no
noi noh-ee we; us
il nome eel nohmeh name
non nohn not
non c'è di che nohn cheh dee keh no problem
non ... per niente nohn ... pehr nee-ehnteh not at all
la notte lah noht-teh night

O

gli occhiali lyee ohk-key-ahlee glasses
oggi ohdjee today
l'oliva *f* lohleevah olive
l'opera *f* lohpehrah opera
ora ohrah now
l'ora *f* lohrah hour; time *(of day)*
l'orologio *m* lohroh-lohjoh watch; clock
l'ottico *m* loht-teekoh optician

P

pagare pahgahreh to pay
pagato pahgahtoh paid
il panificio eel pahnee-feechoh bakery
il passaporto eel pahs-sah-pohrtoh passport

la pasta lah _pah_stah pasta
il pasto eel _pah_stoh meal; dish
la patata lah pah_tah_tah potato
le patatine leh pahtah-_tee_neh French fries
la pellicola lah pehl-_lee_kohlah film *(for camera)*
la pensione lah pehnsee-_oh_neh bed and breakfast
per pehr for; to; in order to
perde _pehr_deh he/she/it loses; you lose *sing. form.*
perdere _pehr_dehreh to lose
perdersi _pehr_dehrsee to get lost; to lose one's way
perdete pehr_deh_teh you lose *pl.*
perdi _pehr_dee you lose *sing. inform.*
perdiamo pehrdee-_ah_moh we lose
perdo _pehr_doh I lose
perdono _pehr_dohnoh they lose
per piacere pehr pee-ah_cheh_reh please
perso _pehr_soh lost
il pesce eel _peh_sheh fish
piace pee-_ah_cheh he/she/it likes; you like *sing. form.*
piacere pee-ah_cheh_reh to like
il piacere eel pee-ah_cheh_reh favor
piacere pee-ah_cheh_reh nice to meet you
piccolo _peak_-kohloh small
il piede eel pee-_eh_deh foot
la pioggia lah pee_oh_-djah rain

la piscina lah pee_she_-nah swimming pool
più pew more
la pizza lah _pee_-tzah pizza
la polizia lah pohlee_tzee_-ah police
il portafoglio eel pohrtah-_foh_-lyoh wallet
possiamo pohs-see-_ah_moh we can
posso _pohs_-soh I can
potere poh_teh_reh can; to be able to
potrebbe poh_trehb_-beh he/she/it could; you could *sing. form.*
potrei poh_tray_ I could
potuto poh_too_toh allowed to; could
il pranzo eel _prahn_tzoh lunch
prego _preh_goh please
prende _prehn_deh he/she/it takes; you take *sing. form.*
prendere _prehn_dehreh to take
prendiamo prehndee-_ah_moh we take
prendo _prehn_doh I take
preso _preh_zoh taken
il primo eel _pree_moh first course *(of a meal)*
pronto _prohn_toh ready
il pullover eel pool-_loh_vehr sweater
può poo-_oh_ he/she/it can; you can

Q

qualcosa kwahl-kohzah something
qualcuno kwahl-koonoh someone
quale kwahleh which
qualè kwahleh which is
quali kwahlee which *pl.*
quando kwahndoh when
quanto kwahntoh how much
il quarto eel kwahrtoh quarter
quello *m* kwehl-loh that
questa *f* kwehstah this
queste *f* kwehsteh these
questi *m* kwehstee these
questo *m* kwehstoh this one
qui kwee here

R

il radiatore eel rahdee-ah-tohreh heater; radiator
la radio lah rahdee-oh radio
il regalo eel rehgahloh gift; present
il riso eel reezoh rice
il ristorante eel reestoh-rahnteh restaurant
rompere rohmpehreh to damage; break
rompersi rohmpehrsee to be damaged
rosso rohs-soh red
rotto roht-toh broken; damaged
la roulotte lah rooloht trailer
il rubinetto eel roobeenehttoh faucet; tap

S

il salame eel sahlah-meh salami; pepperoni
la saponetta lah sahpohnehttah bar of soap
la scarpa lah skahrpah shoe
scusa skoozah excuse me
scusate skoozahteh excuse me *pl.*
Scusi. skoozee Excuse me. / I'm sorry.
Scusi? skoozee Excuse me?
il secondo eel sehkohndoh main course (*of a meal*)
sei say you are *sing. inform.*
la sera lah sehrah evening
il servizio eel sehrveetzee-oh service
lo shampoo loh shahm-poh shampoo
si see one(self)
sì see yes
siamo see-ahmoh we are
la sigaretta lah seegahrehttah cigarette
il soccorso stradale eel sohk-kohrsoh strahdahleh breakdown service
il sole eel sohleh sun
sono sohnoh I am; they are
la spiaggia lah spee-ahdjah beach
sta stah he/she/it is/stands; you are/stand *sing. form.*
lo stadio loh stahdee-oh stadium
stai stah-ee you are/stand *sing. inform.*

Stati Uniti d'America stahtee ooneetee dah<u>meh</u>-reekah United States of America

stare <u>stah</u>reh to be; to stand

stasera stah-<u>seh</u>rah this evening

state <u>stah</u>teh you are/stand *pl.*

stato <u>stah</u>toh been

stiamo stee-<u>ah</u>moh we are/stand

sto stoh I am/stand

subito <u>soo</u>beetoh immediately

suo <u>soo</u>-oh his; her; its; your *sing. form.*

il supermercato eel soopehr-mehr<u>kah</u>toh supermarket

T

la taglia lah <u>tah</u>lyah size *(clothes)*

Tante belle cose! <u>tahn</u>teh <u>behl</u>-leh <u>kohz</u>eh All the best!

tanto <u>tahn</u>toh so much; so many

tardi <u>tahr</u>dee late

te teh you/to you *sing. inform.*

il tè eel teh tea

il teatro eel teh-<u>ah</u>troh theater

il tempo eel <u>tehm</u>poh weather; time

la tenda lah <u>tehn</u>dah tent

ti tee you/to you *sing. inform.*

la toilette lah twah-<u>leht</u> bathroom

la torta lah <u>tohr</u>tah cake; tart

il tram eel trahm tram(way)

il treno eel <u>treh</u>noh train

troppo <u>trohp</u>-poh too; too much

trova <u>troh</u>vah he/she/it finds; you find *sing. form.*

trova: si trova see <u>troh</u>vah he/she/it is located (in)

trovano <u>troh</u>vahnoh they find

trovare troh<u>vah</u>reh to find

trovarsi troh<u>vahr</u>see to be located in

trovate troh<u>vah</u>teh you find *pl.*

trovi <u>troh</u>vee you find *sing. inform.*

troviamo trohvee-<u>ah</u>moh we find

trovo <u>troh</u>voh I find

tua *f* <u>too</u>-ah your *sing. inform.*

tuo *m* <u>too</u>-oh your *sing. inform.*

tutte *f* <u>toot</u>-teh all

tutto <u>toot</u>-toh all; everything

la TV lah tee-<u>voo</u> tv

U

l'ufficio *m* **informazioni turistiche** loof-<u>fee</u>choh eenfohr-mahtzee-<u>oh</u>nee too<u>ree</u>stee-keh tourist information office

un *m* oon a

un' oon a

una *f* <u>oo</u>nah a

l'una *f* <u>loo</u>nah one o'clock

V

va vah he/she/it goes; you go *sing. form.*

vado <u>vah</u>doh I go

vai <u>vah</u>-ee you go *sing. inform.*

vanno <u>vahn</u>-noh they go

vede <u>veh</u>deh he/she/it sees; you see *sing. form.*

vederci veh<u>dehr</u>chee seeing us

vedere veh<u>deh</u>reh to see

vederla veh<u>dehr</u>lah to see her

vederLa veh<u>dehr</u>lah to see you *sing. form.*

vederlo veh<u>dehr</u>loh seeing him

vedermi veh<u>dehr</u>mee seeing me

vedersi veh<u>dehr</u>see seeing oneself

vederti veh<u>dehr</u>tee seeing you *sing. inform.*

vedervi veh<u>dehr</u>vee seeing you *pl.*

vedi <u>veh</u>dee you see *sing. inform.*

vediamo vehdee-<u>ah</u>moh we see

il ventilatore eel vehntee-lah-<u>toh</u>reh fan

il vestito eel veh<u>stee</u>toh dress

vi vee you *pl.*

vicino vee<u>chee</u>noh near, nearby

la videocamera lah veede-hoh-<u>kah</u>mehrah video camera

il vino eel <u>vee</u>-noh wine

il vino bianco eel <u>vee</u>-noh bee-<u>ahn</u>koh white wine

il vino rosso eel <u>vee</u>-noh <u>rohs</u>-soh red wine

la vista lah <u>vee</u>stah view

visto <u>vee</u>stoh seen

il vitello eel vee<u>tehl</u>-loh veal

vogliamo voh-<u>lyah</u>moh we want

voglio <u>voh</u>-lyoh I want

voi <u>voh</u>-ee you *pl.*

volere voh<u>leh</u>reh to want

volete voh<u>leh</u>teh you want *pl.*

vorrei <u>vohr</u>-ray I would like to

vorremmo vohr-<u>rehm</u>-moh we would like to

vorresti vohr-<u>reh</u>stee you would like to *sing. inform.*

vostra <u>voh</u>strah your *pl.*

vostre f <u>voh</u>streh your *pl.*

vostri m <u>voh</u>stree your *pl.*

vostro <u>voh</u>stroh your *pl.*

vuoi voo-<u>oh</u>ee you want *sing. inform.*

vuole voo-<u>oh</u>leh he/she/it wants; you want *sing. form.*

0	1	2	3
zero	**uno**	**due**	**tre**
zehroh	oonoh	doo-eh	treh

4	5	6	7
quattro	**cinque**	**sei**	**sette**
kwaht-troh	cheenkweh	say	seht-teh

8	9	10	11
otto	**nove**	**dieci**	**undici**
oht-toh	nohveh	dee-ehchee	oondeechee

12	13	14	15
dodici	**tredici**	**quattordici**	**quindici**
dohdeechee	trehdeechee	kwaht-tohr-deechee	kween-deechee

16	17	18	19
sedici	**diciassette**	**diciotto**	**diciannove**
sehdeechee	deechahs-seht-teh	deechoht-toh	deechahn-nohveh

20	21	22	23
venti	**ventuno**	**ventidue**	**ventitre**
vehntee	vehntoonoh	vehntee-doo-eh	vehntee-treh

24	25	26	27
ventiquattro	**venticinque**	**ventisei**	**ventisette**
vehntee-kwaht-troh	vehntee-cheenkweh	vehntee-say	vehntee-seht-teh

28	29	30	40
ventotto	**ventinove**	**trenta**	**quaranta**
vehntoht-toh	vehntee-nohveh	trehntah	kwahrahntah

50	60	70	80
cinquanta	**sessanta**	**settanta**	**ottanta**
cheen-kwahntah	sehs-sahntah	seht-tahntah	oht-tahntah

90	100	101	200
novanta	**cento**	**centouno**	**duecento**
noh<u>vah</u>ntah	<u>cheh</u>ntoh	chehntoh-<u>oo</u>noh	<u>doo</u>eh-chehntoh

1000	2000	321
mille	**duemila**	**trecentoventuno**
<u>meel</u>-leh	<u>doo</u>-ehmeelah	treh-chehntoh-vehn<u>too</u>noh

679
seicentosettantanove
say-chehntoh-seht-tahntah-<u>noh</u>veh

Language Tip

Make sure to pay attention to the end vowel between the numbers 20 (*venti*) to 90 (*novanta*). Between 1 (*uno*) and 8 (*otto*) the end vowel of the tens unit is dropped to prevent two vowels colliding, e.g.
venti + uno becomes *ventuno*
novanta + otto becomes *novantotto*.

Monday	Tuesday	Wednesday	Thursday
lunedì	**martedì**	**mercoledì**	**giovedì**
<u>loo</u>nehdee	<u>mahr</u>tehdee	<u>mehr</u>koh-lehdee	<u>joh</u>vehdee

Friday	Saturday	Sunday
venerdì	**sabato**	**domenica**
<u>veh</u>nehrdee	<u>sah</u>bahto	doh<u>meh</u>-neekah